REALITY TV

REALITY TV

Other books in the At Issue series:

REALITY TV

Karen F. Balkin, *Book Editor*

Daniel Leone, *President*
Bonnie Szumski, *Publisher*
Scott Barbour, *Managing Editor*
Helen Cothran, *Senior Editor*

AT ISSUE

OPPOSING VIEWPOINTS® SERIES

GREENHAVEN PRESS®

THOMSON
™
GALE

San Diego • Detroit • New York • San Francisco • Cleveland
New Haven, Conn. • Waterville, Maine • London • Munich

For more information, contact
Greenhaven Press
27500 Drake Rd.
Farmington Hills, MI 48331-3535
Or you can visit our Internet site at http://www.gale.com

LIBRARY OF CONGRESS CATALOGING-IN-PUBLICATION DATA
Reality TV / Karen F. Balkin, book editor.
p. cm. — (At issue)
Includes bibliographical references and index.
ISBN 0-7377-2254-1 (lib. : alk. paper) — ISBN 0-7377
1. Reality television programs. 2. Reality television
I. Title: Reality television. II. Balkin, Karen F., 1949–
Calif.)
PN1992.8.R43R44 2004
791.45'6—dc21   2003055108

Printed in the United States of America

Contents

Introduction

Present almost at the creation of television broadcasting in the late 1940s, reality TV has developed along with the medium and has changed as the nation changed. From the surprised Americans caught in their most embarrassing moments by Allen Funt's *Candid Camera* in 1948, to the down-to-earth Loud family of *An American Family* in 1973, to the rat-eating competitors of *Survivor* in 2002, reality, or unscripted, TV has amused, surprised, and mortified millions of viewers through the years. The changes in program content reflect the changing times: What viewers want to know about the participants as well as what participants allow to be known about them has increased over the years.

For example, post–World War II Americans—new to the nightly entertainment that network television could provide—found the vulnerability of *Candid Camera* participants caught in just a few minutes of embarrassing film to be sufficiently amusing. Different situations with different participants, often in different cities, were aired each week—the audience had no way of knowing what would be shown or who would be on the show. Participants stumbled into embarrassing situations rigged by producers; for example, an unwitting victim might struggle to get a faulty gas pump working, all while the cameras are rolling. *Candid Camera* was good-natured humor, because as Funt said, "[it] caught people in the act of being themselves." While participants might be momentarily embarrassed, their privacy and dignity were protected and no one was hurt. *Candid Camera* competed with half-hour sitcoms and variety programs reminiscent of old vaudeville shows. The country was just getting used to television, and Americans wanted the entertainment that came into their homes to be pleasant, uncomplicated, and not at all controversial.

The relative quiet of the 1950s, with its emphasis on shared conservative values and the sense of moral superiority that came with making the world safe for democracy, came to an abrupt halt when the decade ended. The sexual revolution, the civil rights movement, the antiwar movement, feminism, and drug use were the hallmarks of the 1960s. It was a time of protest against just about everything. Baby boomers, the first generation born after World War II, were just coming of age, and their "tell it like it is" mantra encouraged people to hold nothing back—to debunk old myths and find new truths—in an effort to redefine American culture. As Americans became more sexually open and violent in their behavior, television programs became more sexually explicit and violent as well. By the end of the sixties, openness replaced modesty as a virtue, and independence was more important than privacy.

By the early 1970s viewers who were used to watching Vietnam War footage on the six o'clock news as they ate dinner were ready for more from television—more reality, more invasiveness. *An American Family*, filmed in 1973 by noncommercial public television (PBS), brought TV cameras into the home of Bill and Pat Loud and their family and watched them for seven months as they went about their daily lives. Ten million viewers saw their marriage breakup and heard their son Lance announce for the first time that he was gay. Viewers were willing to accept (some even hoped) that they might be surprised or appalled by what they heard or saw—in part, that was why they were watching. Reality TV let the viewers get to know and identify with the Louds on a long-term basis. Moreover, the Louds had agreed to be filmed, indicating a willingness to be exposed in ways that participants of *Candid Camera* could not have imagined. *An American Family*—unscripted, unrehearsed reality TV—was broadcast as a documentary by a nonprofit network. When the Louds allowed *An American Family Revisited* to document their lives ten years later, it was broadcast on a cable network with millions in paid advertising at stake, and the new show garnered an even larger audience than the original *American Family*. "*An American Family* is widely recognized as the mother of all reality TV shows," claims Jeffery Rouff, a media scholar at Dartmouth University and author of *An American Family: A Televised Life*, a book about the show. By the time a major network developed and produced the *Survivor* series nearly thirty years later, reality TV shows were on almost every channel.

During the first years of the twenty-first century, viewers by the millions were tuning in to watch participants argue, struggle, eat bugs and rats, and reveal the most intimate details of their lives. Reality TV had changed again—this time into a contest where participants competed against each other to win love or money. Competitiveness and materialism were the watchwords of this newest incarnation of reality TV. It reflected, in part, the increased competitiveness in American society. As the new millennium began, it appeared that there was less of everything to go around—fewer good jobs, fewer affordable homes, and, especially, less lasting love. Against this backdrop, the struggles of contestants on reality TV shows to get the girl or win the money made perfect sense. *Survivor* participants secluded on an island were willing to do, say, or eat just about anything to win the one million dollar prize.

Reality TV in the twenty-first century, said Robert Thompson, director of the Center for the Study of Popular Television at Syracuse University, represents "a new way of telling a story which [is] half fiction—the producers and creators set up a universe, they give it rules, they make a setting, they cast it according to specific guidelines as to who they think are going to provide good pyrotechnics. But then they bring in non-actors with no scripts and allow this kind of improvisation like a jazz piece to occur." As reality TV has evolved, *Candid Camera's* harmless embarrassments were superseded by the shameless marital arguing of *An American Family* and ultimately the painful humiliation of those who lost on *Survivor*.

In the past half century, as American television drama has become more violent and sexually explicit and comedy has become edgier, reality TV has also evolved into a genre that many media experts believe presents ever meaner, more competitive, and more hurtful versions of "reality" to an ever-expanding audience. However, many viewers enjoy reality TV. Psychologists offer several interesting reasons for the popularity of the shows: Viewers identify with the ordinary people who are chosen as participants and then become famous; viewers are titillated by the voyeuristic thrill they get from "peeking in"; and they enjoy the competitive nature of the shows—there are always winners and losers. Participants, on the other hand, are attracted to the instant fame that highly rated reality TV shows offer. As one potential participant said, "I just want to get on television. I've had a desire to be famous all my life."

Television networks also like reality TV because it makes them wealthy. Shows with high ratings—reality TV shows were named as twenty of the top twenty-five highest rated shows in 2002—earn millions of dollars in advertising for networks. Moreover, because reality TV shows are unscripted, networks realize huge savings because they do not have to pay writers. For example, it costs about $750,000 per episode to produce a reality TV show; popular sitcoms can run up to $3 million. In fact, producers credit the writers' strike in the spring of 2001 with giving reality TV a boost. Without writers for sitcoms and dramas, producers turned to reality TV shows.

Despite their lucrativeness and popularity, many analysts find current reality TV shows ethically and morally reprehensible. Early reality TV series were good-humored and harmless, they believe, but shows like *Survivor* and its contemporaries are not. Participants can be harmed physically performing various stunts or humiliated and emotionally abused when they fail to win. Further, reality TV shows often glorify superficial characteristics such as physical beauty over spiritual strength and thus set a poor example for teenagers, with whom the shows are especially popular. According to network statistics, twelve- to seventeen-year-olds say that three of their four favorite shows are reality TV shows.

While television producers acknowledge the cyclical nature of television programming—nothing is popular forever—they say they are counting on these youthful viewers to help maintain the viability of a genre that has been popular since the 1940s. "Reality TV allows you to keep your air fresh. It allows you to expand what viewers come to expect from the network," according to Jordan Levin, entertainment chief for the WB network. The current contest-based reality TV shows—*Survivor, The Bachelor,* and *Who Wants to Marry a Millionaire?* among them—appear to have the potential for longevity. "I think it's now beyond a trend," said Robert Thompson, arguing for the permanence of the new reality TV. "It's now a form, just like soap operas, doctor shows, or legal shows. I doubt you, me, our children or our grandchildren will know a time without it." Critics of the new reality TV, however, are hoping that its popularity dwindles. Many, like John Rash, senior vice president and director of broadcast negotiations at the Campbell Mithun advertising agency, yearn for "a return to highly innovative, hard-hitting documentaries and news programs. These were once the hallmark of network TV and have been nearly abandoned," he said.

Whether reality TV ultimately fades into television history or continues to evolve with the medium as a unique genre, for over fifty years it has offered interesting, often controversial entertainment. Authors in *At Issue: Reality TV*, debate the social, psychological, and ethical impact of reality TV as they explore this fascinating aspect of American entertainment culture.

1

Reality TV Has a Positive Influence on Society

James Poniewozik

James Poniewozik, a media and television columnist for Time *magazine, was the media critic and media section editor for the online magazine* Salon.com. *He has also contributed to such publications as* Fortune, Rolling Stone, *and the* New York Times Book Review.

Viewers are tired of seeing bland sitcoms and family dramas on network television and have turned to reality TV for entertainment. Although there are some valid moral objections to reality TV—for example, there is deception involved in *Joe Millionaire*—mostly reality TV is quality satire. Indeed, it ridicules some of the most honored American values like team spirit over individual glorification (*Survivor*) and marrying for love rather than money (*Joe Millionaire*). Further, while many believe that reality TV is harmful because contestants wind up humiliated, in fact, most of the participants are good humored about their failings, which can inspire average Americans to pursue their own dreams. Reality TV benefits society because it teaches that there is nothing more American than to pursue dreams and work for individual improvement.

For eight single professional women gathered in Dallas, it is holy Wednesday—the night each week that they gather in one of their homes for the Traveling *Bachelorette* Party. Munching snacks and passing a bottle of wine, they cheer, cry and cackle as their spiritual leader, Trista Rehn, braves heartache, indecision and the occasional recitation of bad poetry to choose from among her 25 swains. Yet something is unsettling Leah Hudson's stomach, and it's not just the wine. "I hate that we've been sucked into the Hoover vac of reality TV," says Hudson, 30. "Do we not have anything better to do than to live vicariously through a bunch of 15-minute-fame seekers?"

There you have the essence of reality TV's success: it is the one mass-entertainment category that thrives because of its audience's contempt for it. It makes us feel tawdry, dirty, cheap—if it didn't, we probably wouldn't bother tuning in. And in this, for once, the audience and critics agree. Just listen to the raves for America's hottest TV genre:

"*The country is gripped by misanthropy!*"—New York *Observer*

"*Ridiculous and pernicious! Many kinds of cruelty are passed off as entertainment!*"—Washington *Post*

"*So-called reality television just may be killing the medium!*"—San Francisco *Chronicle*

O.K., we added the exclamation points, but you get the idea. Yes, viewers are tuning in to *Joe Millionaire*, *The Bachelorette* and *American Idol* by the tens of millions. Yet, to paraphrase Winston Churchill, never have so many watched so much TV with so little good to say about it.

Well, that ends here. It may ruin reality producers' marketing plans for a TV critic to say it, but reality TV is, in fact, the best thing to happen to television in several years. It has given the networks water-cooler buzz again; it has reminded viewers jaded by sitcoms and dramas why TV can be exciting; and at its best, it is teaching TV a new way to tell involving human stories.

Wallowing in the weaknesses and failings of humanity is a trademark of satire . . . and much reality TV is really satire boiled down to one extreme gesture.

A few concessions up front. First, yes, we all know that there's little reality in reality TV: those "intimate" dates, for instance, are staged in front of banks of cameras and sweltering floodlights. But it's the only phrase we've got, and I'm sticking with it. Second, I don't pretend to defend the indefensible: *Are You Hot? The Search for America's Sexiest People* isn't getting any help from me. And finally, I realize that comparing even a well-made reality show with, say, *The Simpsons* is not merely comparing apples with oranges; it's comparing onions with washing machines—no reality show can match the intelligence and layers of well-constructed fiction.

On a sheer ratings level, the latest wave of reality hits has worked a sea change for the networks. And it has put them back on the pop-cultural map after losing the buzz war to cable for years. Reality shows don't just reach tens of millions of viewers but leave them feeling part of a communal experience—what network TV does best, but sitcoms and dramas haven't done since *Seinfeld* and *Twin Peaks*. (When was the last time *CSI* made you call your best friend or holler back at your TV?) "Reality has proven that network television is still relevant," says Mike Fleiss, creator of the *Bachelor* franchise.

This has sitcom and drama writers praying for the reality bust. "The networks only have so much time and resources," says Amy Sherman-Palladino, creator of *Gilmore Girls*. "Rather than solely focusing on convincing the Olsen twins to allow themselves to be eaten by bears in prime time, I wish they would focus on coming up with something that would really last." TV does seem to be in overkill mode, as the networks have signed up dozens of dating shows, talent searches and other voyeurfests. And like an overheated NASDAQ, the reality market is bound to correct. But unlike earlier TV reality booms, this one is supported by a large, young audience that grew up on MTV's *The Real World* and considers reality as legitimate as dramas and sitcoms—and that, for now, prefers it.

And why not? It would be easier to bemoan reality shows' crowding out sitcoms and dramas if the latter weren't in such a rut. But the new network shows of fall 2002 were a creatively timid mass of remakes, bland family comedies and derivative cop dramas. Network executives dubbed them "comfort"—i.e., familiar and boring—TV. Whereas reality TV—call it "discomfort TV"—lives to rattle viewers' cages. It provokes. It offends. But at least it's trying to do something besides help you get to sleep. Some upcoming reality concepts are idealistic, like FX's *American Candidate*, which aims to field a "people's candidate" for President in 2004. Others are lowbrow, like ABC's *The Will* (relatives battle for an inheritance), Fox's *Married by America* (viewers vote to help pair up a bride and groom) and NBC's *Around the World in 80 Dates* (American bachelor seeks mates around the world; after all, how better to improve America's image than to send a stud to other countries to defile their women?). But all of them make you sit up and pay attention. "I like to make a show where people say, 'You can't put that on TV,'" says Fleiss. "Then I put it on TV."

By and large, reality shows aren't supplanting creative successes like *24* or *Scrubs*; they're filling in for duds like *Presidio Med* and *MDs*. As NBC reality chief Jeff Gaspin says, "There is a little survival-of-the-fittest thing this ends up creating." When sitcoms started cloning goofy suburban dads and quirky, pretty yuppies, we got *The Osbournes*. And now reality TV is becoming our source for involved stories about personal relationships. This used to be the stuff of dramas like the canceled *Once and Again*, until programmers began concentrating on series like *CSI* and *Law & Order*, which have characters as detailed and individuated as checkers pieces. By the time *Survivor* ends, you know its players better than you know *Law & Order's* Detective Briscoe after 11 years. Likewise, the WB's *High School Reunion*, which brings together classmates after 10 years, is really asking whether you're doomed to live out your high school role— "the jock," "the nerd" or whatnot—for life. Last fall two scripted shows, *That Was Then* and *Do Over*, asked the same question but with cardboard characters and silly premises involving time travel. They got canceled. *High School Reunion* got a second season.

"What people are really responding to on these shows is people pursuing their dreams."... A reality show with all humiliation and no triumph would be boring.

In Britain, where reality has ruled Britannia's (air)waves for years, TV writers are starting to learn from reality's success. The sitcom *The Office* uses reality-TV techniques (jerky, handheld camera work, "confessional" interviews) to explore the petty politics of white-collar workers. Now airing on BBC America, it's the best comedy to debut here this season, because its characters are the kind of hard-to-pigeonhole folks you find in life—or on reality TV. On *Survivor* and *The Amazing Race*, the gay men don't drop Judy Garland references in every scene. MTV's *Making the Band 2*—a kind of hip-hop *American Idol*—gave center stage to inner-city kids who would be portrayed as perps or victims on a cop drama.

But aesthetics aside, the case against reality TV is mainly moral—and there's a point to it. It's hard to defend the deception of *Joe Millionaire*—which set up 20 women to court construction worker Evan Marriott by telling them he was a multimillionaire—as hilarious as its fools-gold chase can be. Even the show's Potemkin Croesus contends that producers hid the show's premise from him until the last minute. "The day before I left for France, I signed confidentiality papers which said what the show was about," Marriott tells TIME. "At that point, could I really back out?" Others are concerned about the message of meanness. "There's a premium on the lowest common denominator of human relationships," says James Steyer, author of *The Other Parent: The Inside Story of the Media's Effect on Our Children*. "It's often women degrading themselves. I don't want my 9-year-old thinking that's the way girls should behave."

So *The Bachelorette* is not morally instructive for grade-schoolers. But wallowing in the weaknesses and failings of humanity is a trademark of satire—people accused Jonathan Swift and Mark Twain of being misanthropes too—and much reality TV is really satire boiled down to one extreme gesture. A great reality-TV concept takes some commonplace piety of polite society and gives it a wedgie. Companies value team spirit; *Survivor* says the team will screw you in the end. The cult of self-esteem says everybody is talented; *American Idol*'s Simon Cowell says to sit down and shut your pie hole. Romance and feminism say a man's money shouldn't matter; *Joe Millionaire* wagers $50 million that they're wrong.

The social criticisms of reality TV rest on two assumptions: that millions of other people are being taken in by reality TV's deceptions (which the critic himself—or herself—is able to see through) or are being led astray by its unsavory messages (to which the critic is immune). When a reality show depicts bad behavior, it's immoral, misanthropic, sexist or sick. When *The Sopranos* does the same thing, it's nuanced storytelling. We assume that viewers can empathize with Tony Soprano without wanting to be him; we assume they can maintain critical distance and perceive ironies between his words and the truth. Why? Because we assume that people who like *The Sopranos* are smarter, more mature—better—than people who like *The Bachelorette*.

And aren't they? Isn't there something simply wrong with people who enjoy entertainment that depends on ordinary people getting their heart broken, being told they can't sing or getting played for fools? That's the question behind the protest of CBS's plans to make a real-life version of *The Beverly Hillbillies* with a poor rural family. Says Dee Davis, president of the Center for Rural Strategies, "If somebody had proposed, 'Let's go into the barrio in L.A. and find a family of immigrants and put them in a mansion, and won't it be funny when they interview maids?' then people could see that's a step too far." It's hard to either defend or attack a show that doesn't exist yet, but it's also true that the original sitcom was far harder on Mr. Drysdale [the rich banker in *The Beverly Hillbillies*] than the Clampetts [the hillbilly family]. And on *The Osbournes*, Ozzy—another Beverly Hills fish out of water—was "humiliated" into becoming the most beloved dad in America.

Indeed, for all the talk about "humiliation TV," what's striking about most reality shows is how good humored and resilient most of the participants are: the *American Idol* rejectees stubbornly convinced of their own talent, the *Fear Factor* players walking away from vats of insects like Olympic champions. What finally bothers their detractors is, perhaps, not that these people are humiliated but that they are not. Embarrassment, these shows demonstrate, is survivable, even ignorable, and ignoring embarrassment is a skill we all could use. It is what you risk—like injury in a sport—in order to triumph. "What people are really responding to on these shows is people pursuing their dreams," says *American Candidate* producer R.J. Cutler. A reality show with all humiliation and no triumph would be boring.

And at their best, the shows offer something else entirely. One of the most arresting moments this TV season came on *American Idol*, when a single mom and professional boxer from Detroit flunked her audition. The show went with her backstage, with her adorable young son, as she told her life story. Her husband, a corrections officer, was murdered a few years before. She had taken up boxing—her ring name is "Lady Tiger"—because you can't raise a kid on waitress money. Her monologue went from defiance ("You'll see my album. Lady Tiger don't stop") to despair ("You ain't going nowhere in Detroit. Nowhere") to dignified resolve for her son's sake ("We're never going to quit, are we, angel?"). It was a haunting slice of life, more authentic than any *ER* subplot.

Was Lady Tiger setting a bad example for her son on national TV? Or setting a good example by dreaming, persevering and being proud? *American Idol* didn't say. It didn't nudge us to laugh at her or prod us to cry for her. In about two minutes, it just told a quintessentially American story of ambition and desperation and shrinking options, and it left the judgment to us. That's unsettling. That's heartbreaking. And the reality is, that's great TV.

2

Reality TV Is More than a Fad

Tom Long

Tom Long is a reporter for the Detroit News.

Fads are defined by their ability to attract universal attention—to give diverse people something in common—if only for a short time. America's culture and lifestyle provide the income and leisure time needed to support the development of fads. Moreover, the United States has the complex media mix—television, radio, Internet, movies, newspapers, books, and magazines—required to create fads. While most fads enjoy only brief popularity, reality TV has made a seemingly permanent place for itself in the twenty-first-century American television mix. With its ability to hold the attention of millions of television viewers for several seasons in a row, reality TV is showing itself to be more than a fad.

Tammy Endicott of Ypsilanti [Michigan] has a typically fad-filled life. Her 9-year-old son, Dustin, collects Pokémon cards. She is getting ready to wallpaper the bedroom of her 3-year-old daughter, Samantha, in Power Puff Girls wallpaper. Both of their rooms have cabinets filled with Beanie Babies.

And on Wednesday night, when she wants to relax, Endicott, 29, tunes in to the reality-TV show *Temptation Island.*

"We all talk about it here at work," the medical receptionist says. "I think it's exciting."

Reality TV shows are the hot fad right now. The original *Survivor* hooked millions of viewers last summer [2000] as contestants competed for a $1-million prize on a secluded island. Its successor, *Survivor: The Australian Outback*, was the second-most-watched show. And Fox's *Temptation Island*, which tempts unmarried couples with dream dates, is also getting high ratings on Wednesday nights.

The question is: Is reality TV just a passing fad, such as Pet Rocks or Rubik's cubes, or is it the beginning of something bigger? Rock 'n' roll was called a fad at first. But after some 50 years, it's moved from fad to fashion to being an ensconced part of our culture.

Robert Thompson, professor of pop culture and media at Syracuse University, remembers sitting in front of a bank of TV sets last summer showing a wide variety of TV networks, and they were all discussing *Survivor*.

"That's what makes a fad," Thompson says. "It's on everybody's radar screen."

Reality TV has what it takes to be with us for a long time. "This is going to become part of the mix of what we see in American television."

Thompson says he thinks reality TV has what it takes to be with us for a long time. "This is going to become part of the mix of what we see in American television," he predicts.

In recent decades the pace of fads has accelerated: Teenage Mutant Ninja Turtles to Smurfs, prime-time game shows to prime-time reality shows, Puka shells to Pogs.

"We never ask what's going to be the next fad, because it's there before we're looking for it," says Mike Bernacchi, professor of marketing at University of Detroit Mercy.

There is a variety of reasons why fad culture has been growing for most of the past century. One is quite simple—"We have the income to do it," Bernacchi says. Plus we have the leisure time. So even though most fads have a quick burnout rate, we are consistently drawn to these pop culture spasms, to fads we know will probably disappear within a year.

Fads give people something in common

"People apparently genetically have to have something to group around," says Ray Browne, professor emeritus of pop culture at Bowling Green University in Ohio. "Fads are temporary, momentary efforts to find something in common."

Which means there actually was some logic behind the Beanie Babies craze and the hula hoop. Flagpole sitting and marathon dancing. Zoot suits and conga lines, and goldfish swallowing. In the mid-'30s, 20,000 people lined up outside Macy's department store in New York in hopes of buying a Buck Rogers Disintegrator Ray Gun. In the early '50s, kids wore beanie caps with propellers on top. Five years later any boy who didn't have a Davey Crockett coonskin cap was a social outcast.

As technology has grown, so has the speed at which fads take hold.

"One hundred years ago, the fads in New York didn't come to us in Ohio until 18 years later," says Bowling Green's Browne. "The speed with which we congregate is much greater now."

"We have this extraordinary sophisticated media complex which allows for a mechanism to create fads," says Syracuse's Thompson.

The Internet, cable TV, satellite dishes, magazines, radio, newspapers—they're all just waiting to let us know about the latest fad the instant it happens.

And right now, reality TV has everyone's attention. While the jury's still out, strong ratings for the second season of *Survivor*, as well as *Temptation Island* could help make these shows as common as sitcoms. Meanwhile, the true fads will just keep coming.

"The human being is so motivated to get outside his own personal society and do something with a crowd that it is probably a very healthy and safe thing," Browne says.

Tammy Endicott is well aware of the social basis for fads. Her son Dustin collects Pokémon cards, because "they're just something to be kind of in with their friends," she says. "A lot of it's just to be with the cool guys."

Browne says, "It's a pressure valve.

"Fads are normal and natural ways to relieve the pressure. And to enjoy life.

"Come on," he says. "These things are fun!"

3

The Terrorist Attacks on America Diminished the Popularity of Reality TV

Kim Campbell

Kim Campbell is a staff writer for the Christian Science Monitor.

Since the September 11, 2001, terrorist attacks on America, people find watching reality TV too stressful and are therefore turning to sitcoms and comedies for entertainment. They are uneasy with the conflicts and unpleasant competition portrayed in reality shows and want to watch programs containing less anger and danger.

W hen Americans go home at night now, they are looking for comfort—especially in the form of their favorite TV shows.

Forget about new fall [2001] programs and reality series. The equivalent of tomato soup to viewers right now is the predictable haplessness of "Raymond" [a popular sitcom] and the question of paternity for Rachel's baby on "Friends" [a popular sitcom].

Uneasy with the news of the day, people want programs in which conflicts are resolved in an hour and the next joke is only a commercial away. They prefer story lines that don't incorporate the [September 11, 2001, terrorist attacks] and some even draw the line at anything dark.

"I don't even want to watch 'ER' [a hospital emergency room drama] anymore," says Kathy Kennedy, a 20-something who works in Boston and prefers sitcom "Will & Grace." "Anything that's sad or dramatic . . . it seems too much of a reality."

In recent weeks, shows that once landed squarely in the Top 20—such as "Who Wants to Be a Millionaire"—have been bumped lower on the list in favor of seasoned programs such as "The West Wing" [a dramatic show]. Reality programs like ABC's "The Mole" and Fox's "Love Cruise" have been at the bottom of ratings for the . . . two weeks [following the 9/11 attacks], leading some observers to believe the format may not be compatible with the current climate in the nation.

"What people want in their prime time shows . . . is escapism," says Joan Giglione, a lecturer in communication at California State University at Northridge. "They want something that takes them away from stress, that takes them away from danger—where reality TV puts it right in their face."

Moviegoers are looking for familiar faces

Cultural observers say the same thing is happening with movies, where familiar faces such as Michael Douglas are reigning at the box office, along with thrillers that offer closure in the space of an afternoon. But one of the biggest tests of current tastes is coming tonight [October 11, 2001]—when the third season of "Survivor" goes up against "Friends."

This fall marks the first time reality shows are scheduled as part of the regular lineup on major networks, rather than replacements for failed programs or off-season fillers. Poor performance by such shows might have happened without Sept. 11, with market saturation and uneven quality. But some observers say the attacks couldn't help but have an effect.

"Sept. 11 erodes the appeal of reality programming. I don't think it destroys it," says Neal Gabler, author of "Life: the Movie." A big draw of these shows was suspense, he says. Now, "suspense is the last thing we want. We live in suspense."

"[People] want something that takes them away from stress, that takes them away from danger— where reality TV puts it right in their face."

Polls taken since the attacks bear out that claim, with only 17 percent of 500 respondents saying they'd be likely to watch reality programs, and 57 percent saying they would watch comedies, according to a survey by Initiative Media taken Sept. 21 to 23.

Television viewers talk about having no patience now for shows that involve backstabbing, when the country is trying to work together, or trivial matters such as couples hooking up. "I find the people on them whiny and self-involved," says Jessica Auger, another Boston 20-something. For her, comfort in recent weeks has come from watching "Law & Order"—another Top 20 show.

Historically, after major events—like the assassination of President [John F.] Kennedy—people eventually returned to their pre-tragedy preferences, says Mr. Gabler. "People were traumatized, but it didn't mean we didn't watch the gun play anymore," he says. "We overestimate the impact of a single event on culture."

4

The Ultimate Reality TV Show: Coverage on the War in Iraq

Michiko Kakutani

Michiko Kakutani is a Pulitzer Prize–winning book critic for the New York Times.

Network producers have turned real-time reporting of the 2003 war in Iraq into prime-time reality TV entertainment. Rather than presenting the real horror of the war, newscasters are discussing the conflict as though it were a movie. Producers are engaging in willful sensationalism and sentimentality in an effort to keep viewers from changing channels or not watching at all.

A decade or so after the Vietnam War ended, in the wake of a legion of Vietnam movies, some veterans put bumper stickers on their cars that read, "Vietnam was a war, not a movie." They did not want people to forget the losses that they and their comrades had sustained during the war. They did not want people to relegate their memories of that bloody and divisive war to flickering images on the silver screen.

With the new engagement in Iraq, however, the Pentagon and television news coverage are blurring the lines between movies and real life as never before, turning viewers into 24-hour couch voyeurs.

In the opening days of the war the focus on television was almost entirely on the fireworks spectacle of the American air attack on Baghdad . . . and on heroic and often unrepresentative images that deliberately recalled photographs and famous cinematic sequences: soldiers planting an American flag in Iraq with Iwo Jima–like determination; caravans of troops driving across the desert, made famous by "Lawrence of Arabia"; a soldier tearing down a billboard of Saddam Hussein while video cameras rolled and smiling Iraqis looked on.

There were fewer images thus far on American television of the painful costs of war. While much of the world from the Middle East to the

Philippines had seen videotape of American prisoners of war, broadcasters in the United States initially elected not to show these scenes, and the networks said they would probably never broadcast the full version of the tape. American television showed little tape of Iraqi civilians affected by the bombing of Baghdad and little of the sometimes fierce resistance American, British and Australian forces are meeting.

The start of the war [March 19, 2003] caused business at movie theaters to drop by 25 percent on Wednesday as people stayed home to watch the war, and snack-food sales and restaurant deliveries thrived. The opening salvos of the war had taken the place of prime-time entertainment, and television stations did their best to serve up gaudily produced coverage: the war in Iraq as the ultimate in reality television, as the apotheosis of every favorite Hollywood genre, from the combat thriller to the coming-of-age tale to the blow-'em-up, special-effects extravaganza.

As he watched the "shock and awe" bombing that lighted up the Baghdad sky on Friday [March 21, 2003], the veteran reporter Peter Arnett exclaimed, "An amazing sight, just like out of an action movie, but this is real." . . . Other commentators and viewers were drawing a lot of movie analogies too.

Comparing the war to movies

The burning oil-well fires elicited comparisons to science-fiction movies; the plight of seven Tennessee families who had sent pairs of fathers and sons off to the war brought comparisons to "Saving Private Ryan." Allusions to the HBO miniseries "Band of Brothers" were ubiquitous, and the postbombing videotapes of [Iraqi leader Saddam Hussein] (which might have starred one of his doubles) drew comparisons to the comedy "Dave," in which a look-alike fills in for an ailing American president, and "The Prisoner of Zenda." Even the Iraqis got into the act: In the days before the war, Iraqi television played music from the movie "Gladiator" to rally Baghdad residents.

The war in Iraq [is shown] as the ultimate in reality television, as the apotheosis of every favorite Hollywood genre.

References to the movies also occurred in the aftermath of the terrorist attacks of Sept. 11 [2001] planned by media-savvy Al Qaeda operatives who presumably knew how their acts would play on television around the world. But in that case, the comparisons with "Independence Day" and "Towering Inferno" were expressions of people's inability to get their minds around the horror, their failure to find real-life precedents for what they had seen.

There is an element of this inability on the part of eyewitnesses to the war, but there is also an element of willful sensationalism and sentimentality on the part of producers who want to keep viewers from switching channels. As for Pentagon planners, who have had a longtime alliance with Hollywood and who spoke of their "shock and awe" campaign in terms of high-tech special effects, they hoped from the start to present a sanitized view of the war, a strategy inevitably foundering.

In the hour before President George W. Bush's ultimatum to Saddam expired, cable channels ran ticking clocks on their screens, the same sort of clock that ABC would later use in counting down to the Oscars.

After Friday's air assault on Baghdad, television anchors took to promising viewers that there was more "shock and awe" to come, and military analysts talked about how new technology had made the Pentagon "more imaginative than it's been in the past" and "more creative." It all might have been a trailer for the disaster movie "The Core," due for release this month [March 2003], in which the Colosseum in Rome and the Golden Gate Bridge in San Francisco are destroyed with special effects. But it may be recalled that many television networks, including ABC, CBS, CNN and Fox, are owned by multimedia corporations well practiced in the manufacture of entertainment.

Happy-talk anchors, more accustomed to talking about DKNY [Donna Karan New York, a fashion design company] and MTV, giddily tossed around terms like "MOAB" (Massive Ordnance Air Blast, or the "mother of all bombs") and "BDA" (bomb damage assessment), while fashionistas debated who was this war's hottest Scud Stud and Studette. ABC featured computerized graphics called "Virtual View," which took the audience on video-game-like tours of Iraq from the air. Fox ran exclamatory headlines like "The Ultimate Sacrifice" and "Weapons Scandal."

Because the impulse to blur the lines between the real and the fictional is so potent, newscasters repeatedly reminded audiences that the scenes of the war they were seeing weren't a movie. But coming in the midst of television's razzmatazz coverage of the war, those reminders felt like those coy titles at the end of docudramas: "This was based on a real story." In this case, reminders are meant to give the audience a racy frisson of danger, rather than a sober appreciation of the solemn business of war.

5

Fascination with Fame Attracts Reality TV Viewers

Steven Reiss and James Wiltz

Steven Reiss is a professor and James Wiltz is a doctoral candidate at Ohio State University.

Reality TV viewers do not watch the shows so they can talk about them with their friends. Nor is it true that those who watch reality TV are less intelligent than those who do not or that viewers watch hoping to see illicit sex. Devoted reality TV watchers enjoy the competitive aspect of the shows—the concept that there are winners and losers. But the most significant reason that reality TV is popular with such a wide variety of viewers is that Americans identify with the desire to be famous. Even if the fame is touched with infamy—contestants are not always shown in a favorable light—viewers believe that being watched by millions means that the participants are important.

E ven if you don't watch reality television, it's becoming increasingly hard to avoid. The salacious *Temptation Island* was featured on the cover of *People* magazine. *Big Brother* aired five days a week and could be viewed on the Web 24 hours a day. And the *Survivor* finale dominated the front page of the *New York Post* after gaining ratings that rivaled those of the Super Bowl.

Is the popularity of shows such as *Survivor, Big Brother* and *Temptation Island* a sign that the country has degenerated into a nation of voyeurs? Americans seem hooked on so-called reality television—programs in which ordinary people compete in weeks-long contests while being filmed 24 hours a day. Some commentators contend the shows peddle blatant voyeurism, with shameless exhibitionists as contestants. Others believe that the shows' secret to ratings success may be as simple and harmless as the desire to seem part of the in crowd.

Steven Reiss and James Wiltz, "Why America Loves Reality TV," *Psychology Today*, vol. 34, September/October 2001, p. 52. Copyright © 2001 by *Psychology Today*. Reproduced by permission.

Rather than just debate the point, we wanted to get some answers. So we conducted a detailed survey of 239 people, asking them about not only their television viewing habits but also their values and desires through the Reiss Profile, a standardized test of 16 basic desires and values. We found that the self-appointed experts were often wrong about why people watch reality TV.

Two of the most commonly repeated "truths" about reality TV viewers are that they watch in order to talk with friends and coworkers about the show, and that they are not as smart as other viewers. But our survey results show that both of these ideas are incorrect. Although some people may watch because it helps them participate in the next day's office chat, fans and nonfans score almost equally when tested on their sociability. And people who say they enjoy intellectual activities are no less likely to watch reality TV than are those who say they dislike intellectual activities.

Reality TV allows Americans to fantasize about gaining status through automatic fame.

Another common misconception about *Temptation Island*, a reality program in which couples were enticed to cheat on their partners, is that the audience was watching to see scenes of illicit sex. Some critics were surprised that the show remained popular when it turned out to be much tamer than advertised. In fact, our survey suggests that one of the main differences between fans of the show and everyone else is not an interest in sex but a lack of interest in personal honor—they value expedience, not morality. What made *Temptation Island* popular was not the possibility of watching adultery, but the ethical slips that lead to adultery.

Competition is important

One aspect that all of the reality TV shows had in common was their competitive nature: contestants were vying with one another for a cash prize and were engaged in building alliances and betraying allies. The first *Survivor* series climaxed with one contestant, Susan Hawk, launching into a vengeful tirade against a one-time friend and ally before casting the vote that deprived her of the million-dollar prize. It makes sense, then, that fans of both *Survivor* and *Temptation Island* tend to be competitive—and that they are more likely to place a very high value on revenge than are other people. The *Survivor* formula of challenges and voting would seem to embody both of these desired qualities: the spirit of competition paired with the opportunity for payback.

But the attitude that best separated the regular viewers of reality television from everyone else is the desire for status. Fans of the shows are much more likely to agree with statements such as, "Prestige is important to me" and "I am impressed with designer clothes" than are other people. We have studied similar phenomena before and found that the desire for status is just a means to get attention. And more attention increases one's sense of importance: We think we are important if others pay attention to us and unimportant if ignored.

Reality TV allows Americans to fantasize about gaining status through automatic fame. Ordinary people can watch the shows, see people like themselves and imagine that they too could become celebrities by being on television. It does not matter as much that the contestants often are shown in an unfavorable light; the fact that millions of Americans are paying attention means that the contestants are important.

And, in fact, some of the contestants have capitalized on their short-term celebrity: Colleen Haskell, from the first *Survivor* series, has a major role in the movie *The Animal*, and Richard Hatch, the scheming contestant who won the game, has been hired to host his own game show. If these former nobodies can become stars, then who couldn't?

The message of reality television is that ordinary people can become so important that millions will watch them. And the secret thrill of many of those viewers is the thought that perhaps next time, the new celebrities might be them.

6

Reality TV Exploits Fame Seekers

Rochelle Riley

Rochelle Riley is a columnist for the Detroit Free Press.

Reality TV has proven that people will do just about anything to be on television and be made famous, even if it is only for a few minutes. However, people who are made "famous" by having their most intimate conversations overheard by millions of TV viewers stand to lose more than just their privacy—they have surrendered their self-respect as well.

It is painfully obvious, based on the general direction of American television, that the most coveted thing in America truly is that elusive 15 minutes of fame we all grow up wanting, and, as lore holds, we are due at some time.

There's the current crop of TV shows based on fear and stamina and a bachelor and bachelorette looking for love in all the wrong places (in front of millions); there's the public heartbreak of auditioning for a mad Englishman just so he can tell you the obvious, that you can't sing, all to become an "American Idol." And then, there's ABC Family's "The Last Resort," last year's [2002] miniseries that comes back this year [2003] as a full-blown series. Nine couples will go into seclusion in beautiful Hawaii and decide whether to make up or break up (with millions watching).

The couples are required to devote seven days to the taping. Here's hoping the show doesn't last seven seasons.

It has finally happened. Reality TV has jumped the shark. The reality boom that has become the new millennium's casting couch, the latest way to get a TV or film contract, has passed entertainment.

After all, there sure is something sad about couples trying to strengthen or demolish their partnership by arguing on TV. The whole concept seems to be at odds with the idea of sharing your most intimate secrets, dreams and beliefs with just one person at a time.

Fame is not enough

We are all one step from stardom, whether we are singers or actors or writers or potters. With every moment in our offices and every year of our lives, we wonder whether we've done something that shows the rest of the world our worth, our character, our potential, our brilliance.

Then we move on to the next task, forgetting for a moment that the 15 minutes eluded us again. But it will eventually creep up again, that feeling that we should be doing something more important.

We search, not always for fame, but for some sense of legacy, of people knowing we were here after we're gone.

Sometimes we want more than the typical headstone, love of family, appreciation of a company.

But do we really want that lasting impression to be our disappointed faces on national TV when a bachelor gives the roses or necklaces to the other girls in the room?

Do we really want our big moment to be a public date with several other people and a few cameras along?

It is painfully obvious, based on the general direction of American television, that the most coveted thing in America truly is that elusive 15 minutes of fame.

Is it so important that we'll eat cow manure or jump off a building just so someone can say, "Hey, didn't you almost kill yourself on 'Fear Factor'?"

The answer, increasingly, is yes.

My sense that there's too much reality on TV doesn't apply to the public talent shows. That's show business. I watch "Star Search" and "American Idol" and root for the amateurs who jump into a spotlight they want to own. I wonder whether I'm seeing the next Michael Jackson.

Unlike "Star Search" and "American Idol," which are plain and simple auditions, "The Last Resort" is the last step before that old television staple, "Divorce Court." It's that painful place where wrenching conversations are had and promises are made. What would make someone take those delicate, intimate negotiations to such a public forum? It's that elusive 15 minutes of fame.

But in the end, the only thing the couples might gain is the derision of future mates and a headstone that, instead of saying "Devoted Wife," says "Devoted Fame-Seeker" and instead of "Devoted Husband" might say "Drew 5 million viewers."

7

Reality TV Participants Enjoy Fame and Success After the Show Is Over

Jonathan Storm

Jonathan Storm is a columnist and TV critic for the Philadelphia Inquirer.

Many past participants in reality TV shows find that fame follows them after the shows are over. Some contestants are able to stay in show business and find jobs hosting various programs on cable channels. Many are well paid for personal appearances or have been hired to host local TV or radio shows while other reality TV personalities use their fame to do charitable work. However, the majority of reality TV veterans know their fame cannot last forever and realize that they will have to go back to reality someday.

Things aren't working out for "Survivor" veteran Jenna Lewis in her new office job.

"You're really weird," her boss explains as he fires her. "The show is over. You don't need a camera crew following you around."

"But I like it," she whimpers.

It's a scene from "Survivin' the Island," a hilarious short film starring Lewis, the ninth person voted off the island in the original "Survivor," as herself. (You can catch it at www.ifilm.com.) As with all good satire, it underlines reality.

It's also the first film that satirizes an unseen component of reality TV. Contestants who have traveled to the ends of the Earth to reveal their inner selves to millions of strangers are discovering that life after reality can be one strange trip.

"We really had no idea," Lewis said in a phone interview. "I have had a great adventure for the last two years."

Some found fortune. Some maintained their fame. Like the outcome of the programs themselves, a lot depended on luck. Veterans of the early "Survivor" episodes are doing best at manipulating the limelight. Competitors from other broadcast-TV reality shows are having a tougher time.

Colleen Haskell, cuter than a bunny even when bugs ate into her legs, co-starred last summer [2001] in the Rob Schneider movie "The Animal." She was scheduled to play the girlfriend of the reprobate brother on the WB sitcom "Maybe It's Me" on Friday night. Hardcore "Survivor" fans could have switched when it was over to see her fellow contestant Kelly Wiglesworth hosting a special on cable's E!

Elisabeth Filarski, from "Survivor II," was not the only one to land her own TV series, but, on the Style Network's "The Look for Less," she's the only one who gets a cable network to help her shop for clothes. Her cast-mate Keith Famie hosts a taste-and-travel show on the Food Network. Original "Survivor" crusty curmudgeon Rudy Boesch has turned himself from a drydocked Navy Seal into an entertainment conglomerate with a book and a succession of TV shows. He now hosts USA Network's "Combat Missions."

Like almost all "Survivor" survivors, million-dollar man Richard Hatch gets big paychecks for personal appearances. But he has also been hired as a morning radio personality in Boston. He's not the only one. Other Survivors have landed jobs on local TV news shows.

Straight-talking Susan Hawk figures her run after "Survivor" has so far earned her what she would have made in six years in her old job driving trucks. She has moved from Wisconsin to Las Vegas, primarily for her husband's health. In the gambling mecca, she combines real-world business with showbiz razzmatazz. [Early in April 2002], she closed a deal to buy Juices Wild, a smoothie shop she plans to run herself. The next day, she shot a Dockers ad that will air internationally, beginning in June 2002.

Alumni of other reality shows, on the air for brief segments, as in NBC's "Fear Factor," or in more obscure venues such as Fox's "Temptation Island," have had less luck.

William "Will Mega" Collins vanished into obscurity after making a racial fuss when booted from "Big Brother" nearly two years ago. Justin Sebik, the man who took a knife to one of his "Brother" cohabitants last summer [2001], is out on bail after being arrested in January [2002] and charged with assaulting his girlfriend. Alumnus Bill "Bunky" Miller was kicked out of the Christmas parade in his North Carolina hometown because the mayor and an influential pastor objected to his homosexuality.

Mandy Lauderdale, the red-headed vixen from "Temptation Island," lost her father [late in March 2002]. He was 51, diagnosed with liver cancer in December [2001]. But she's moving on with her career—she and her rock band, Ragdoll, are moving from Florida to L.A.

Saddest of all is the story of Angel Juarbe. On Sept. 4 [2001] he emerged as the $250,000 survivor/winner on Fox's low-rated "Murder in Small Town X." One week later, the New York firefighter was killed in the terrorist attack on the World Trade Center.

Show business attracts many reality TV vets

Some of them have agents. Some have publicists. Some have managers. Some have all three.

"I'm not too happy about it," said Ethan Zohn, mop-topped heart-throb of millions, who won the $1 million on "Survivor III." He said he had hired an agent "when I realized I just couldn't handle all the incoming calls."

Zohn, the former pro soccer goalie who has been hired by sponsor Philips Electronics to cover the U.S. team from Japan during the World Cup in summer [2002], still shares a two-bedroom apartment with two roommates in a less-than-tony Manhattan neighborhood. Like most of his "Survivor" class, he's enjoying the parties, but doing very little paying business, primarily because the demand has dried up as the reality buzz has subsided.

"People have gotten wary about hiring a reality-TV personality," said Lewis, who, like many of her confreres, has moved to Los Angeles, showbiz central. "We were being thrown everything when we first came off, and now it's like they don't dare touch you."

Reality vets seeking acting careers have been dissociating themselves from their bug-eating, wilderness past.

Colby Donaldson, who finished second on "Survivor II,' is incommunicado, studying acting in Los Angeles. Haskell, and even Hatch, are extremely choosy about "Survivor" publicity.

Others continue to tout their "Survivor" resumes.

Contestants who have traveled to the ends of the Earth to reveal their inner selves to millions of strangers are discovering that life after reality can be one strange trip.

Kim Powers is back in the Philadelphia area. She has a manager ("Doesn't that sound cool?") who made sure she met all the right people while she was judging the recent Miss USA contest. And she just returned from a promotional event in Las Vegas for Coors beer and Zima, a citrus-flavored malt liquor. Famous folks including Charles Barkley mingled with distributors and other assorted suds professionals.

Powers, 5-foot-1, stood on a step to be seen. "I was so intimidated. There were so many major celebrities. I thought, 'No one's going to come and ask for my autograph.'

"There was a huge line!"

Gervase Peterson is concentrating on acting and writing TV treatments. He and a partner have written a comedy, a dramedy, a drama and a movie they're shopping around. "We have a whole Wednesday-night lineup," he said with a grin. (But where's the reality show?)

Peterson estimates that the pay for a personal appearance such as Powers' Las Vegas gig starts at $2,000 a day and can climb past $20,000, depending on the type of event. He says he still does one every month or so.

His "Survivor I" castmate Gretchen Cordy learned the value of a smile and a signature.

"Initially, I was doing a lot of high-paying things and traveling a lot, speaking engagements—$3,500 for an overnight deal," she said.

"I couldn't make that much if I was a hooker."

Cordy has landed at least one step up from that profession. She's a morning radio personality in her hometown of Clarksville, Tenn. (population 100,000). She says that two months after "The Q Wake-Up Crew With Jack and Gretchen" debuted, it was No. 1 in the market.

Two other Survivors have bigger broadcasting jobs. Alicia Calaway ("Survivor II") is the new health-and-fitness reporter at New York's Fox 5. Neurologist Sean Kenniff ("Survivor I") is health correspondent at CBS's WFOR/4 in Miami and member of a medical team that serves CBS affiliates nationwide.

Those two got their jobs through more or less normal channels. By contrast, Cordy was offered hers after the station manager heard her speak to a local gathering of Big Brothers Big Sisters of America.

Many of the reality vets do charities, with emphasis on the personally relevant. Tina Wesson, who downplayed her religious beliefs while winning "Survivor II," has spent much of her post-TV time speaking to Christian organizations. Joe Baldassare and Bill Bartek, the gay "Team Guido" of "The Amazing Race," say they work extensively for anti-AIDS and human-rights charities. Peterson, whose mother has developed Alzheimer's disease, does fund-raising events for the Alzheimer's Association of South Jersey.

Lewis, a single mother of two, said: "If I can help at any time, being a pseudo, Grade B celebrity, I'm ready."

The charity work puts some meaning in the post-reality circus.

"When it's all said and done, we're dancing bears," said Joel Klug from "Survivor I," who has had parts in several TV shows, including "Nash Bridges" and "Baywatch"; done an independent movie; and made scores of high-paying personal appearances. He estimates that he could take in $1 million before it's all over.

"None of us really went looking for this whole life," Klug said, "but how dumb would we be not to capitalize on it?"

And when it's over?

"I don't know what I'm going to do," Lewis said. "I'll have to get a job and leave the world of reality TV and go back to reality."

8

Reality TV Can Offer a Positive Religious Message

Jill Terreri

Jill Terreri is a reporter for the Niagara Gazette, *which is published in Niagara Falls, New York.*

The immorality and negativity of conventional reality TV can be countered by the religious reality show *TruthQuest*. Positive Christian virtues such as friendship, trust, faith, and hope are emphasized in the show as a vehicle for enjoying life and having fun as well as doing good work. While most reality TV shows are popular because they offer viewers a chance to see participants in compromising situations, *TruthQuest* depends on the drama created by Christian teenagers who proselytize in areas where they are not welcome.

A group of teenage missionaries will be featured in a new "reality" television show that turns the tables on the genre. "TruthQuest: California," which will be shown beginning Oct. 3 [2002] on FamilyNet Television, a cable Christian television station reaching 34 million homes, thinks its good clean Christian fun can succeed. Others doubt it.

Richard Sparkman is only 14, but he has already worked as a missionary. [In 2001] he visited New Orleans with his Franklin, Tennessee, church's drama troupe to spread the gospel by performing skits.

But [in 2002], his family will be able to keep a close eye on Sparkman as he evangelizes with other teenagers along California's coast. Sparkman, an eighth-grader at Freedom Middle School, will be featured in "TruthQuest: California," the brainchild of Todd Starnes of Baptist Press—the national news service of the Southern Baptist Convention. The series will be shown . . . on FamilyNet, a Christian-oriented cable television network. FamilyNet reaches 34 million homes, the same amount of combined households that subscribe to HBO and Cinemax.

Starnes said he was channel surfing and noticed MTV's "Road Rules," a show in which seven strangers travel in a Winnebago and are given clues at each stop that indicate their next destination. He said that even though that show was racy there were themes that, as an evangelical Christian, he could relate to.

"I noticed that at the end, they were using basically spiritual concepts, talking about friendship and trust and faith and hope, and it just got me thinking," Starnes said. "If these guys can use spiritual concepts in that kind of a setting, why can't we do the same thing from a Christian point of view?"

Twelve teenagers were selected for the show, most of whom were strangers to each other. In July [2002], the group participated in team-building and whitewater rafting on the Ocoee River in eastern Tennessee before they headed west.

The drama of Christian teenagers proselytizing in places where they may not receive a warm welcome will carry the show.

Viewers will be able to watch the group as they work at a community center in San Francisco, try to convert surfers in San Diego and evangelize to those along the way on a 1,200-mile, 16-day journey.

The students range in age from eighth-graders to seniors in high school. All of the teens come from Southern Baptist churches and have had prior missions experience.

Freeman Field, 17, came to the attention of the show's producers when Starnes traveled to New York City after [the September 11, 2001, terrorist attacks] and interviewed him for *Baptist Press*.

This reality show promotes Christian values

Field was a senior at Stuyvesant High School, a Manhattan public high school located two blocks from the World Trade Center site. Field wrote a personal account of the attacks and their aftermath for a Christian teen magazine.

Field is relatively experienced, as young missionaries go. He has already traveled to Texas, Kentucky and North Carolina on missions. He also has done volunteer work at Ground Zero [site of the collapsed World Trade Center towers], feeding relief workers.

Field is hoping that the program will show teenagers in a positive light. "I think that by having a reality show with a positive value system, it would just be refreshing, and show that all teenagers aren't crazy," he said. "We can kind of be a role model for other kids to see."

Other participants echoed Field's hopes.

"I was watching 'Road Rules' a couple days ago and all they do is argue and have sex," said Sarah Brown, 16, of Youngstown, Ohio. "I'm a teenager; I argue with my parents, but I don't have sex all day. It's not reality TV.

"People need to see that not every teenager has a foul mouth, or is out there being promiscuous or smoking. You know we actually do positive things."

Shanna Hawkins, 17, of Winston-Salem, North Carolina, said she is eager to show the world the fun side of being a Christian.

"I am hoping that they'll get a glimpse that there are teenagers in the world who are Christians, and also who know how to have fun," she said.

But that very cleanliness could work against the show's ability to attract viewers. The show will lack the key element that draws viewers to reality shows: the chance to see the participants in compromising situations.

This curiosity is the main reason viewers watch reality shows, said Ted Baehr, an analyst for the Christian Film and Television Commission, an organization that evaluates media content for Christian families. Without that more racy content, it's harder to get teens to "tune in," he said.

Another strike against the show is that reality television may be an idea whose time has already gone, Baehr added.

"The worst thing you can do is jump on a bandwagon, because by the time you jump on it, it's already left," he said, conceding that the idea "could work" against all expectations.

But Starnes believes that the differences between *TruthQuest* and the others will work in its favor.

He is hoping that the drama of Christian teenagers proselytizing in places where they may not receive a warm welcome will carry the show.

"We want people to know that Christians don't just go to church 24/7, but that they are engaged in their culture," he said.

Some Reality TV Shows Encourage Cooperation

John Kiesewetter

John Kiesewetter is a TV and radio critic for the Cincinnati Enquirer.

Most reality TV shows emphasize competition and divisiveness and make a mockery of teamwork and cooperation. However, a reality show reenacting the 1770 voyage of Captain James Cook from Australia to Jakarta, Indonesia, using forty volunteer sailors, proves that reality TV can encourage positive virtues such as cooperation, helpfulness, and selflessness. The grueling thirty-five-hundred-mile journey aboard a replica of Cook's eighteenth-century ship required that crew members work effectively with each other at all times—the verbal abuse common in other reality TV series would have made the level of cooperation necessary aboard the ship impossible. Instead of working against one another to win an individual prize, crew members learned to work together to reach the common goal of a successfully completed voyage.

A Carnival cruise it wasn't. There was no hanky-panky for these TV shipmates.

Forty volunteers sailed from Australia aboard a replica of Capt. James Cook's *Endeavour,* to experience six weeks on an 18th century sea voyage.

The History Channel calls this co-production with the BBC a "history adventure reality series."

"The Ship" . . . is a little "Frontier House," a little "Survivor" and a lot of hard work.

"The physical labor was difficult," says Cole Smith, 47, an Oklahoma prosecutor who had no sailing experience.

"For just a crewman like myself, I had no idea how fast we were going. I had no idea where we were on the planet, other than in a big body of water," Smith says of the ship that sailed about 3,500 miles from the northeast coast of Australia to Jakarta, Indonesia.

Capt. Cook, the first European to reach Australia, traveled that route in 1770 as part of his three-year voyage.

Crew member Cyril O'Neil, 30, of Los Angeles, wasn't very impressed with the 109-foot vessel also dubbed "The Ship." He probably saw more glamorous structures on Hollywood movie sets.

"When I set foot on the ship, I actually thought: This thing is a tub, and we'll never make it," says O'Neil, who coordinated all the vehicles seen in the film "American Pie II."

"It's not people trying to knock each other down. It is . . . just the opposite. It's people trying to figure out how we can work together, to get where we need to go."

Four Americans were among the cast and crew. Also aboard: a goat (for milk), chickens (for eggs), 15 professional sailors, cooks and navigators, and 18 miles of rope.

All worked and lived as 18th century sailors, but they didn't wear period costumes. Crew members slept in hammocks 14 inches apart under the ship's deck.

The crew learned to work as a team

They learned to climb the 130-foot mast to unfurl the sails. They worked as a team to pull up the anchor.

Unlike Cook's vessel, or PBS' "Frontier House" cabins, "The Ship" had some modern conveniences—a satellite phone to summon emergency medical help for a sick British crew member, and a flush toilet in the lower deck for use while sailing in the Great Barrier Reef. On the open seas, the sailors used the "seat of ease," essentially a wooden toilet seat mounted over the bow.

Women also were aboard, another difference from Cook's 100-man crew. The only American woman on "The Ship," Melissa Smisko, 28, a Washington, D.C., financial consultant, used the "seat of ease" when the toilet broke. Overall, the voyage wasn't as bad as she feared.

"I mentally prepared myself for the worst," she says. "I really mentally prepared myself to be filthy all the time . . . possibly hungry all the time. So I was pleasantly surprised.

"Yes, I was dirty. Yes, I was hungry. Yes, I was tired. (But) it wasn't as bad as I was prepared for," she says.

The History Channel also provides a glimpse back in time through readings from Capt. Cook's journals, dramatized by reenactors.

"It is very much the story of two adventures, the 18th century adventure and the 21st century adventure," says Chris Terrill, the film's producer, director and cameraman. "We weren't trying to be 18th century people. . . . We were very manifestly 21st century adventurers going in the footsteps of these historical characters."

Like "Survivor," "The Ship" is a cinematic pleasure, full of beautiful aerial shots and colorful sunsets. But in contrast to CBS' popular reality game show, everyone on "The Ship" pulled on the same rope at the same time.

"What will set this show aside from a lot of other reality television shows is that . . . we all set out as a group to see if we could do what 18th century sailors did," O'Neil says. "And that gave us a purpose other than trying to outsmart . . . your enemies to win a million bucks.

"It's not people trying to knock each other down. It is, in fact, just the opposite. It's people trying to figure out how we can work together, to get where we need to go," O'Neil says.

The trip back in time without TV, e-mail and the Internet was a life-altering experience for Smisko.

"I didn't miss any of it, and I was very happy, even with only three T-shirts and three pairs of shorts," she says.

"I've really become much less of a consumer, and I've really tried to simplify my life."

Doesn't sound like she will book a Carnival luxury cruise any time soon.

10

Reality TV Encourages Racial Stereotyping

Cary Darling

Cary Darling is an entertainment writer for the Miami Herald.

The portrayal of black men on reality TV is stereotypically racist. Black men are shown as either angry and violent, lazy and stupid, or sexually aggressive and dominating. Reality TV shows do not show a wide spectrum of black men—educated, uneducated, athletic, quiet, or politically active—but depend on a few predominately unpleasant types for representation. Further, there is rarely more than one black male participant at a time on a reality show, no matter how many races are represented. Due to the pervasive nature of racism in America, producers of reality TV shows may not even be aware that they are seeking stereotypes when they choose black male participants. However, that is no excuse for allowing racial stereotyping to continue.

The explosion of so-called reality TV this summer [2000] has America buzzing about issues of avarice, privacy and the tantalizing taste of rat-fried rice. But these new shows also highlight a dilemma that has long stalked the genre. The title of a recent Internet bulletin board post summed it up best in one line of mock incredulity: "What's Up with the Black Guys?"

The note, posted by someone named Imelda on www.realworldblows.com, bemoaned the image portrayed of young black men on highly rated shows like "Survivor" (a group of people thrown together on a deserted island, eating rats), "Big Brother" (ditto, except it's a house, no rats), "The Real World" (ditto, except it's a really nice house) and, by extension, "The Real World's" nomadic cousin, "Road Rules" (ditto, except it's a Winnebago).

"Does anybody else think it's weird that on all three of these dumb shows ("RW/Surv/BB"), the black guys are being portrayed as total unconforming pains-in-the-ass . . .?" writes Imelda. "I mean, one or two are OK, but three out of three as examples of black male dysfunction seems a little hard to swallow."

Written before housemates and viewers made Will, the lone black man rattling around that claustrophobic inner sanctum known as "Big Brother," the first to be "banished" from his show, the posting sparked debate on race and image. But the issue is hardly new. As a black guy, I've long been peeved with reality TV's portrayal of black men.

Don't get me wrong, I'm neither player-hater nor P.C. [politically correct] killjoy. I realize audiences for these shows desire to see four things: fights, sex, back-stabbing and more fights. I love a good knockdown, drag-out televised brawl as much as the next guy. Nobody wants to watch a "Real World" with seven Colin Powells [African American secretary of state] prattling about foreign policy; that's why God created C-Span. And the whites on these programs—from the bare-chested, boozy battlers on "Cops," the original reality show, to scab-caked Puck on "The Real World"—aren't exactly going to be beating [physicist] Stephen Hawking to the podium to pick up that Nobel Prize either.

Still, considering fictional TV and film's troubled history regarding racial issues, it's bothersome to see black men once again straitjacketed as either nitroglycerin explosive, fatcat lazy, mack daddy randy, or some combination of the three. (Conversely, the images of black women have been more even-handed.)

• 1992: In the debut season of MTV's "The Real World," set in New York, racially conscious and contentious Kevin is accused of throwing a candlestick at one of his white roommates, Julie. (Cameras weren't present, so it's a case of his word against hers.)

• 1993: In the show's second season, in L.A., David is the first cast member to get kicked out of "The Real World" "phat pad" because his roughhousing gets out of hand and the women in the cast feel threatened.

• 1997: Syrus, from the Boston edition, makes the moves on anything wearing an approximation of a skirt and brings lots of women back to the house.

• 1998: Stephen, in the Seattle "Real World," is forced to go to anger management sessions after slapping housemate Irene.

• 1999: As for Teck, from the Hawaiian "Real World," well, see Syrus above.

• 2000: William, from "Big Brother," is booted from the house because of his perceived hostile and confrontational attitude; Gervase, from "Survivor," admits on the show that he does no work and is the laziest castaway (his remarks sparked a comedic rebuke from black humorist David Alan Grier on CBS-TV's "The Early Show" the following day); difficult David, from the current New Orleans season of "The Real World" and, to a lesser extent, loverboy Laterrian, from the current "Road Rules," seem to be trying to rip a page from Syrus and Teck's bulging "booty call" handbook.

Granted, some of the resulting confrontations make for "good TV," and the subsequent arguments about race sometimes inject a needed sense of the outside world into these prefabricated realities. And there have been exceptions to the stereotypes—Mohammed from San Francisco's "The Real World," Kefla from "Road Rules Australia," Shawn from "Road Rules Semester at Sea" come to mind—but that doesn't alter the overall image. As there seems to be a limit of just one black guy per cast, it ends up falling on him to "represent," and the pattern is unmistakable.

"This is very much happening," says Robert Thompson, director of the Center for the Study of Popular Television at Syracuse University in New York. "The big question is what's driving it."

For their part, producers of such shows have long denied any conscious stereotyping along group lines. "We don't have a formula," "Real World/Road Rules" co-creator Mary-Ellis Bunim said to me in a 1998 interview. "We go into this looking for seven interesting people from diverse cultures (who) have an interest in learning something from each other. It's their life experience, not the color of their skin, the experience with their parents, how they relate to the opposite or the same sex."

As a black guy, I've long been peeved with reality TV's portrayal of black men.

Others aren't so sure. "I honestly believe the people who do the screening look for the angry black male, or the player, the savage African," says Bruce Britt, a cultural columnist for *Code*, an L.A.-based fashion/lifestyle magazine aimed at young black men. "I can't help but notice stereotypes in TV in general. You have all these shows like 'Felicity,' 'Dawson's Creek' and '90210' that portray white boys as very sweet, concerned and contemplative. But when it comes time to cast a black person, they always play up the image of the angry black man.

"I'm always hearing about the 'rage of the black man.' I'm not constantly enraged, and a lot of the things that enrage me aren't necessarily race-oriented," he says. "I might be offended by a lot of things—the proliferation of boy bands—but my rage doesn't always focus on white people. It's some conceit of theirs: 'Look at them. They can't stop thinking about us.'"

For his part, Thompson allows the stereotyping may not be conscious. "These kinds of racist issues are so pervasive in American society that people with perfectly good intentions still continue to perpetuate them," he says.

Stereotypes are the easy way out

As with fiction, these reality programs crave conflict and resolution, heroes and villains, and so fall back on easily recognizable types. A multichannel universe where itchy fingers operate the remote controls may not be the place for subtlety; it may be easier to retreat into deeply embedded cultural codes.

Stuart Fischoff, professor of media psychology at California State University, Los Angeles, points to "Big Brother" as a big example. "For all intents and purposes, you have the very smart, enterprising Chinese person, you have the rather vapid white beauty queen, you have the black woman who is the strong mother type and you have the guy with one leg who is kind of brittle. You have the Midwest 'Aw shucks' kind of plump Pillsbury dough boy father figure, you have the exotic dancer and you have the angry black man.

"There may well have been other black people who applied but they weren't as edgy as William," Fischoff continues. "We tend to see (people in other groups) as much more similar to each other than we see our own in our group. You see William and that's your typical angry black man. If you'd see the white guy do the same thing as Gervase, you'd say he's just a lazy guy. If someone like Black Entertainment Television does it with eight blacks and two whites, you'd have the reverse effect. You'd have all sorts of different people and you'd have this white schnook."

Other groups may not be amused by their portrayals, either. "It isn't just black people who are watching," Fischoff says, referring to "Survivor" castaways Richard (gay, portrayed as Machiavellian) and Stacey (female attorney, portrayed as bitchy). "It's gays and lawyers, too. I have a number of gay friends, and they are watching Richard on 'Survivor' very, very closely. A lot of them are humiliated or embarrassed about how he behaves."

Certainly, for all the producers' wiles, they can't create an image if the "actors" don't give them something to work with. This has been acknowledged by Kevin Powell, the black male housemate from the first "The Real World." It was his black female housemate of the time, Heather, who made it clear for him. "Heather said they basically used what we gave them. What are you going to do?," he told me in a 1997 interview after his book, "Keepin' It Real: Post-MTV Reflections on Race, Sex, and Politics," was published. "Obviously, it's not just me, but (fellow cast members) Norman, Becky and Andre were all typecast. I'm more than the angry black male, and I've grown since then, too."

Thompson and Fischoff both contend that these real people share in the blame for the way they are portrayed. "This is a screen test," Thompson says. "They're trying to be famous, trying to guarantee magazine close-ups for themselves. To an extent, some of these people may be playing into stereotypes themselves."

Perhaps, but it would be refreshing, if only for the change of pace, if it were the black guy who remains culturally conscious but is the parasailing athletic one, the bookish studious one, the politically conservative one, the weirdo spacey one, or the boy next door instead of being the ticking bomb or the lusty Lothario. (Or, heaven forbid, that they have two very different black guys on one show.)

"We have come such a long, long way, but we also have come a very, very short distance," says Marilyn Kern Foxworth, a former professor at Florida A&M University who has studied media stereotypes for three decades and is now the first African-American female president of the Association for Education in Journalism and Mass Communication. "We don't think every African-American person on TV should be a doctor, but there should be a balance. If you're going to have an angry black male, you also need to have a black male who has gone to school and has a different view, who is not angry, who is saying it's rough out there and we have to work harder but we can make it."

'Nuff said. Now pass that rat filet over here.

11

Reality TV Is a Dangerous Art Form

Ben Alexander

Ben Alexander is a New York playwright and the author of Jocelyn, *a play about a young woman contestant on a reality-based TV show.*

Reality TV is a dangerous mix of fantasy and reality. In fictionalized drama, real people do not get hurt, but in reality TV shows, despite the fantasy situations, participants—real people—can get hurt. What is worse, as viewers grow bored with the genre, the stakes will need to be raised. Reality TV participants will have to be put in increasingly greater physical and emotional peril in order for viewers to stay interested.

Two women meet. They come from sharply contrasting backgrounds, there's an age difference, and the setting isn't quite conducive to forming intimate bonds; still, they bond. They find themselves becoming close friends, sharing much with each other and feeling increasingly connected. Yet, in the situation that has brought them together, as well as in their own individual characters, lurk the seeds of their friendship's destruction. The younger woman presently makes a choice which, though it makes sense toward achieving her cherished goal, totally offends and infuriates the other, and a warm relationship is swiftly replaced by bitterness and hurt.

Thus, before the audience, unfolds the drama in the play "Collected Stories," by contemporary American dramatist Donald Margulies. The audience sees a young fiction-writing student come under the tutelage of a renowned novelist, and watches as the teacher-pupil rapport turns into a friendship. In the course of that friendship, the teacher shares much of her early life experiences with her pupil. The teacher also teaches the pupil, get ideas for your fiction writing from wherever you can. Well, thanks to her good teaching, the young woman gets a book of short stories published to critical acclaim. But if she wants to be taken seriously as a fiction writer, she's eventually going to have to write a novel. Trouble is, she's lived such a sheltered life, she's got nothing to write a novel about, except . . . yep, you guessed it, she makes a novel out of her teacher's early life, the stories her teacher has told her in the course of their friendship. There's a final scene in which the teacher, devastated and enraged as well as terminally ill now, dismisses her former friend from her life and sits alone in her apartment, soon to die.

If the script and the performance are working right for you, you're going to feel sad at the end. You will have developed an identification with both characters in the course of the two hours, and you will experience the emotional impact of that final scene. In fact, you may well express how good it was by saying something like "I cried like a baby," or, if you didn't like it, you may express it by saying "It didn't move me."

This, indeed, is what drama is all about, in the many forms in which it comes. Whether it's "Saving Private Ryan," "One Life to Live," "Law and Order," "King Lear," whatever, the point is, when you meet the characters and get to know them, you expect to start to care about them, and then, as they find themselves in dangerous or troublesome situations, you experience emotions on their behalf. You worry about their welfare. You cry when things fall apart for them. You foam at the mouth at the villains who mean them harm. And, when they face weighty moral dilemmas, you feel proud of them if they make the more honorable choice, and disappointed if they sell out.

What does it take for drama to move us? What *is* drama? First and foremost, I would say, drama is about personal relationships. Drama shows characters with their need for love and intimacy (encompassing the romance, family, and friendship varieties). It's usual, in fact, for a story to feature one central personal relationship, with the main suspense being about where that relationship is going to end up. And, generalizing even further, it is not at all uncommon for that relationship to be threatened by one or both parties having other needs that get in the way. In the example above, for instance, the young woman's need for the friendship gets eclipsed by her need to publish a novel.

What makes [reality TV] particularly dangerous, particularly endangering, is that it has the stakes of reality alongside the disinhibitions of fantasy.

(This is not, of course, the only common formula for relationship-centered drama. Another very effective scenario is that a relationship develops and/or strengthens under adverse external conditions, such as an oppressive power structure, with the tragedy that oppression sometimes makes it too late to learn lessons and grow. We see this with a marriage in Arthur Miller's "The Crucible" and with a gay male liaison in Martin Sherman's Nazi-Germany drama "Bent.")

So, drama tends to focus on a personal relationship and the challenges of sustaining it, and it tends, if it's effective, to evoke human emotions as audience members develop their sense of caring about this relationship. When a drama is working for you, you are *worried* about the main characters, hoping they'll come out all right, hating the antagonists who mean them harm, and suffering grief when they do come to harm.

What does it take to create a drama that will produce these effects? It takes a whole range of skills that playwrights are trained in and practice over time. Job one is creating characters. Each individual character is expected to seem real and believable, and the combination of characters should be such as would naturally lead to some conflicts and dangers. Since the audience does not want to watch people agreeing on everything, you don't give them characters who will. And, when plotting out the conflicts that will arise, those conflicts are expected to flow naturally out of the characters as they've been presented, and the stakes are expected to be high. You don't write a two-hour play in which a husband and wife have lost their opera tickets and are looking everywhere for them. Well, actually, let me qualify that. Maybe you will write such a play, but brother, sister, there'd damn well better be more at stake, ultimately, than whether they find those opera tickets. When I'm in playwriting workshop groups, I constantly hear playwrights advise each other to "raise the stakes" in the situations they've created.

Relationships. Conflicts. Dilemmas. Stakes. Emotions. Ideas. These elements are found in drama and in audiences' response to it.

Reality TV is the ultimate drama

Now, let's revisit what we started with, the scenario of the making and unmaking of a two-woman friendship. In the summer of 2000, a lot of American TV viewers saw that played out, not in any Donald Margulies play, but on "Survivor," with the legendary Sue and Kelly. There was a big difference from most drama, though: Sue and Kelly were real. In "Collected Stories," you're watching two actresses. Right after their bitter scene, they're going to come out on stage, join hands, and bow, then perhaps go to a nearby bar and have drinks together for the next two hours. Not so with Sue and Kelly. When Sue told Kelly she'd feed her to the vultures, she meant it. She was no actress.

What makes reality TV the ultimate drama for some people is precisely the fact that the stakes *are* real. The hatred between Sue and Kelly was real. The tension between Shannon and Bunky (and between Shannon and just about everybody else in that "Big Brother" house, not including Will of course) was real. On "Temptation Island," the relationships that may break up are real. And yet, *and yet*, what's missing, compared with normal real life, are the inhibitions. In the normal world, people sharing a house do try their best to get along. (Does anybody have reason to doubt that Cassandra, of [Big Brother 1], keeps the peace and promotes civility in her off-screen friendship and family circles? By that logic, she was *very* real in that house, though not everybody found her particularly entertaining.) In the normal world, people in committed relationships don't go looking for an affair, nor are they surrounded by an army of seducers for such. In the normal world, people's lives just aren't all that dramatic, in the conventional stage sense.

Therefore, reality TV producers have to combine reality with some manipulation of circumstances. They pick some extreme personalities and they encourage extreme behavior. Believe me, it's no accident that these shows tend to have somebody whom you'll "love to hate." The selection is deliberate. They also pick combinations likely to have some sparks. I suspect Shapiro would have preferred to have Shannon and Nicole together for longer, to let the audience see a protracted, engaging catfight. And there's enough of an element of make-believe, of artifice, to bring out the most uninhibited behavior. I'd say this is particularly true of "Temptation Island." The behavior, especially of the tempters, is anything but real: They are acting. And yet, at the same time, the relationships that are in danger of being broken up—*are real!*

In fact, if drama requires danger, at least emotional danger, something for the viewers to be worried about, in order for it to be effective, then it stands to reason that reality TV is about setting up real danger, real endangerment, to produce that effect. And if most drama has some kind of antagonist, reality TV has to set up some people to appear in that role. What makes it particularly dangerous, particularly endangering, is that it has the stakes of reality alongside the disinhibitions of fantasy. Justin on "Big Brother 2" was probably able to feel that he wasn't a monster, just playing one on TV. Ditto for the tempters on "Temptation Island": "I'm not a homewrecker (or, one might add, slut), I just play one on TV!"

Well, in the traditional kind of drama, that distinction is clear. I recently asked "Temptation Island" fans on a message board whether they would enjoy seeing their daughters as temptresses on there. The consensus was that no they wouldn't. Now, I might also have asked, how would you feel about seeing your daughter play Abigail Williams in "The Crucible"? She has an affair with a married man, then charges the man's wife with witchcraft, and ultimately is instrumental in getting the man, who rejected her and stood up for his wife, hanged. Would you want your daughter playing such a role? I think most people would reply, "Silly question! It's acting, it's not real!" Therein lies a key difference between the way audiences perceive conventional drama and reality TV. And yet, as long as their own daughters aren't in the line-up, they will get themselves quite caught up in the drama of which couples will break up and which newly formed pairs will do the nasty on the island.

But here is what makes reality TV potentially more dangerous than is realized in the present season. There is a principle, understood well by marketers, that a product needs to get more intense and more novel in order to sustain and expand its market. Just as movies today require more action and blood and guts to attract large audiences than they did in the early twentieth century when the form was still novel, and just as producers can get away with a lot more intensity now than they could before, it may well be that reality shows in the future are going to require higher emotional stakes, and viewers will actually be expecting—and getting—on-air nervous breakdowns and hurtful behavior leading to suicide. And such consequences, perhaps, will be seen as little worse than a knee injury in football.

You can't have drama without stakes, you can't have stakes without danger, and you can't sustain reality TV without drama. Put that all together, and it is precisely because of the principles of drama that reality TV is an extremely dangerous art form, and one which, if it continues to flourish, can be expected to become a lot more dangerous.

12

Reality TV Violates the Public Trust

John C. Dvorak

John C. Dvorak is a contributing editor for PC Magazine. *His work appears in several magazines and newspapers, including* Boardwatch, Computer Shopper, *and* MicroTimes, *and he is the author of several books on computers, including* Dvorak's Guide to Telecommunications.

The public was led to believe that the reality TV series *Joe Millionaire* was a legitimate documentary. Television advertising and newspaper articles insisted that the show was real—unrehearsed and unscripted. Only the Internet hinted at the truth, suggesting that Joe was not who he claimed to be and that women on the show were actresses. When it was revealed that the show was actually a hoax and that Joe was not a millionaire but a construction worker, the public trust was violated to a degree that demanded Congressional investigation. If *Joe Millionaire* or any other reality TV show is scripted or prearranged in any way, Congress should investigate it as it investigated rigged game shows in the 1950s. The public trust is at stake and should not be violated for the sake of ratings.

H as the Internet become the only way we can get a glimpse at facts? I think so more and more, despite all the hoaxes and fakery there. On the Net, at least you have a shot at finding out the truth.

My journey into the vagaries of truth begins with the Fox reality TV show, "Joe Millionaire." This is a show where a normal guy poses as a millionaire to fool a bunch of gold diggers who are trying to win the contest by becoming the last gal standing in an elimination game. We are told this is all real. This, to me, looks to be a somewhat scripted hoax, along the exact promotional lines of *The Blair Witch Project*, with actors playing both ad-libbed and scripted roles in a false documentary. But you would never even suspect this by reading the daily papers. Only the Internet gives us a clue.

If this show can be proven to be a false documentary, by the way, then it seems like a clear violation of the public trust—one much like that highlighted in Congressional hearings regarding the fifties game show "21" on which Charles Van Doren was given the answers to quizzes and coached on how to react. If it wasn't okay to buffalo the public then, but is okay today, what changed? Remember, this is TV, not the movies.

The possibility of "Joe Millionaire" being a fake began to emerge when one of the finalists—Sarah—turned out to be an actress who has appeared in bondage films. This was supposed to be a scandal, but nothing has been made of the fact that the other finalist, Zora Andrich, is also an actress! You need only a few swipes at the Internet to find this out. Dig deep enough, and you'll likely discover that her agent got her the job on the show. Other girls got the job from casting calls. That's how one of the other contestants, Alison, won the job, as reported January 3 [2003] in *The New York Post* (now off-line, but available in a Google cache). Alison is a "part-time" actress (isn't everyone?) who went to a casting call for the job.

The show is convincing as reality only if you suspend disbelief. And perhaps you can credit the producers with a touch of genius for producing a drama that is actually made to seem like a documentary. The greatest drama of this type, and the one that had the biggest impact, was Orson Welles' "War of the Worlds," a radio play written in the form of a music show with news flash interruptions heralding an alien invasion. It was brilliant, and perhaps "Joe Millionaire" is brilliant too. But if it's a hoax, can we ever believe that any reality TV is real? Worse, there is a public trust issue here that is seriously in need of Congressional attention.

Before I delve more deeply into the public policy issues, I want to outline some aspects of the show that logically indicated to me that it was scripted. Sarah has been playing the bad girl throughout the last few episodes, baiting her friend Melissa M about the fact that she makes out with Joe Millionaire (Evan) at every turn. Two weeks ago on the show, Sarah took Evan into the woods to ditch the cameramen and make out. But, omigod, Evan and Sarah left their wireless microphones on and we heard all sorts of grunting and groaning. This occurred right after he asked her to lie down. Now I can tell you from experience that just sitting down without the wireless transmitter pack digging into you is difficult enough. Rolling around without noticing the thing and turning it off would be unlikely.

That said, the next week this same girl gets dropped off at her hotel room and decides to sneak into Evan's room afterwards. She just has to see him. So she pounds on the door. She could have called, of course, but no, she pounds. And golly, she's all miked up and the camera boys, who I guess were sleeping in the hall, catch it all on tape. It stretches credibility. To be honest, I haven't seen all the shows (ugh) but the ones I have seen are riddled with dubious situations.

Web sites tell the real story

The Internet was the first place you found skepticism about all this, and some of what's going on here looks like part of a bigger scheme. Again, *The Blair Witch Project* pseudo-documentary—promoted through real-looking Web sites related to the film's story line—comes to mind. The Web site called JoeMillionairre claims to blow the lid off the whole scam.

The Perry site says the show is a total fake, and offers to tell you who really wins, to collect your e-mail address. When you get the e-mail it says the winner is Melissa M—who was eliminated the week before. Then you see that the e-mail is filled with legal disclaimers saying that the Web site and the mail are "for entertainment only . . ." blah, blah, blah. Very suspicious.

Then there is the underground group of gay gossip sites and forums that claims that the star, Evan, is a male escort and model living in Southern California. He may have worked as a construction worker at one time or another, but who hasn't? One of the contestants, named Mojo, coincidentally has the same name as another porn actress, Mojo or Mojo Hunter. When you try to find pictures of the porn actress, you discover that many are suddenly obscured. None of this is immediately obvious from watching the show, since the women do not give out their last names, and we are left with what sound like stage names for lap dancers: Dayana, Mandy, Brandy, Melissa Jo. Even with little information to go on though, using Google turns up all sorts of interesting items.

Can we ever believe that any reality TV is real? Worse, there is a public trust issue here that is seriously in need of Congressional attention.

But are any of these dubious aspects of the Joe Millionaire show revealed to us by the daily papers or the TV newscasts? No. With the exception of the one story about Sarah being a bondage film actress, we hear nothing but promotional fluff. We know nothing about any of these people, even though they do get interviewed left and right in puff pieces written as news. And even *The New York Post* plays along with the game, leading the public to believe that this is all legit and, oh my, that those poor women were fooled by the phony millionaire.

There is always the possibility that Fox will come clean and that there is supposed to be a twist at the end of the show other than the one where Joe Millionaire tells the girls he's not rich. The Internet is abuzz with theories like this, including those speculating that we'll be told the entire show was a hoax. Won't that be funny? Ha ha. What next? Fake newscasts about nuclear war? Why not, if the money is good?

Two years ago, one of the contestants, Stacey Stillman, in the TV show Survivor sued CBS for fraud, saying the show was rigged. The case is still pending, and the poor woman got sued in return. You can read an eye-opening deposition online. I had a long chat with Donald Yates, one of the attorneys for Stillman, and he said that the worst part about all this was that neither the FCC [Federal Communications Commission] nor any government bodies showed any interest. It was depressing, he said. "It's not the nineteen fifties anymore, nobody gives a sh— about any of this."

Maybe nobody does care. But the fact that the news organizations have become nothing more than lapdogs for the entertainment industry is beyond pathetic. In fact, if "Joe Millionaire" is scripted in any way, this is a breach of the public trust that should be investigated by Congress the same way the fake games shows were investigated. This is television, not movies. The media companies and the news organizations should be brought up to testify. The public is already too cynical and doesn't know what to believe. We're becoming Sovietized. We have to read gossip on the Net to have a hint at what might be going on. This is not right. Send this column around, and let's see if we can shake up our drowsy Congress—see if they do "give a sh—" or not.

13

Reality TV Helps Young People Learn About Life

Kimberly Shearer Palmer

Kimberly Shearer Palmer is a graduate student at the University of Chicago.

Young people find reality TV instructive as well as entertaining. They learn about dating, relating to their families, and dealing with sensitive issues such as AIDS, cancer, and mental illness by watching the way reality TV show participants deal with these crises. Because reality TV is unscripted and unrehearsed, the situations portrayed reveal true feelings and the realistic consequences of actions—good and bad.

Our obsession began with weekly dinners at which we would scrutinize the eligible men on ABC's *The Bachelorette*. My twentysomething friends and I debated which man would best suit our own needs as well as Trista's [participant on *Bachelorette*]. After celebrating her final choice, we thought we needed a new evening activity. We were wrong. Despite the relative lack of emotional depth of Fox's *Married by America*, we've already picked out our favorite and least-favorite candidates.

Critics of reality shows aren't wooed as easily. Some psychologists have even argued that programs such as ABC's *Are You Hot?* contribute to eating disorders. But reality TV also comes with a slew of benefits.

Just as our parents watched *American Bandstand* to learn how to dance, we snuggle up to today's reality shows because they give us a sense of how people date, relate to their families and deal with sensitive issues. The pre-makeup, frizzy-haired versions of people's lives on reality programs have a lot to teach us.

While some, such as *Are You Hot?* and Fox's *Temptation Island* seem merely titillating, many reality programs cover the consequences of sex better than fictional shows. In real life, negative consequences can't be written out of the script. When teenage Julia got pregnant in a 1996 episode of Fox's fictional *Party of Five*, she had a miscarriage before she had to decide whether to have an abortion. In reality, quick fixes don't often come so easily. On MTV's *The Real World,* viewers watched as one housemate, Pedro Zamora, died from AIDS in 1994.

Vicky Rideout, a vice president of the Kaiser Family Foundation, says Zamora's death "had a huge impact on awareness about AIDS. . . . It put a human face on that disease."

Shows shed light on safe sex and disease

Reality shows can teach safe sex by showing a range of attitudes and their consequences. On Fox's *American Idol,* Frenchie, a promising contender, was dropped after producers learned she had appeared on an Internet pornography site. *Joe Millionaire* finalist Sarah was ridiculed after viewers learned she had appeared in bondage videos—a sharp contrast with the winner, the apparently innocent Zora.

Reality shows also offer an informative look at diseases, partly because producers can't control which ones strike their characters. Herman Kattlove, a medical oncologist at the American Cancer Society and adviser to such shows as NBC's *Days of Our Lives,* says that for fictional shows, "An empathetic character is a 17-year-old with leukemia. . . . Colon and lung cancer aren't popular"—even though they are far more common and kill more Americans than any other cancer.

Reality TV reflects this. Sharon Osbourne, co-star of MTV's *The Osbournes,* underwent treatment for colon cancer. She appears to be recovering well—a valuable lesson in cancer's treatability, Kattlove says.

We snuggle up to today's reality shows because they give us a sense of how people date, relate to their families and deal with sensitive issues.

When they see sugarcoated dramas, cancer "survivors say, 'It didn't look like that when I had it,'" says American Cancer Society spokesman David Sampson. "But this is the real deal. We welcome reality television. . . . (It) strips away the mystery of cancer."

Reality TV also can demystify psychiatric conditions and underscore that many people face such issues yet live normal lives. *The Bachelorette's* "studly" Jamie talked openly about his panic disorder; Trista assured him it wasn't why she rejected him.

Reality TV catches the blemishes and scars behind the thick makeup that coats fictional dramas. When those blemishes include the risks of unsafe sex, cancer treatment and mental illness, viewers are left with the realization that most people, after all, don't live the romanticized lives of NBC's *Friends.*

Still, even the real world isn't filled exclusively with skin breakouts and bad hair days. Reality TV also brings hope of second chances: Frenchie, the contestant kicked off *American Idol,* was hired by *Entertainment Tonight* to cover [the April 2003] Grammy Awards.

14

Teenagers Identify with the Issues Presented in Reality TV Shows

David Hiltbrand

David Hiltbrand is an entertainment writer for the Philadelphia Inquirer.

Teenagers prefer to watch reality TV shows because they are attracted to the relatively short duration of reality TV series. Further, reality TV shows often deal with relationships and rejection, two issues with which teenagers typically identify. Teens' preference for reality TV has led networks to shift their programming in that direction since advertisers—particularly those in certain product categories such as movies, soft drinks, and cosmetics—prize youthful viewers. Networks now realize that teenage viewers are trendsetters, and that the programs they like often turn out to be the most successful.

If your television could talk, it might fill you in on the real generation gap in this country—the gulf between what teenagers like on TV and what everyone else is watching.

An analysis of ratings information for the current TV season shows that teens have distinctive viewing habits. In fact, 14 of the top 25 shows among 12- to 17-year-olds are nowhere to be found among the top 25 shows for all viewers. Nearly half of the most popular teen shows air on Fox.

And the epidemic of reality programming? To a great extent, you can blame it on teens. They can't get enough of the tawdry stuff. Shows such as "American Idol" are helping arrest a precipitous decline in network ratings among adolescents.

Above all, teens like to laugh. Comedies account for more than half of their top 25. Only three dramas made it onto the teen list: "CSI" (No. 12), "Smallville" (17), and "7th Heaven" (20).

The overall top 25—a list dominated by adult choices—is far more sober, laden with 10 dramas, from "CSI" (No. 1) to "JAG" (24). Those longer shows may help explain why grown-ups watch far more TV than young folks do.

As for reality shows, they hold down three of the top four slots for the teen group. Those viewers' appetite for such programming extends to such otherwise marginal offerings as "Fear Factor" (No. 14 for teens) and "Celebrity Mole: Hawaii" (24). These shows rank 32d and 46th with the overall audience. [In early March 2003,] the younger audience for "Fear Factor" boosted NBC to its first victory over an original episode of CBS' "Everybody Loves Raymond" (No. 9 with all ages) in nearly four years.

What accounts for this disparity in viewing tastes?

Clearly, it is in part a matter of age. But today's teens are also growing up in a far more varied and alluring entertainment environment than previous generations—a world offering endless video games, the Internet, and hundreds of cable channels.

As a result, says Betty Frank, executive vice president of research for MTV Networks, "they're used to getting what they want when they want it. So they're impatient. They move around a lot. They have short attention spans."

The limited duration of reality series, which typically last between four and 13 weeks, enhances their teen appeal. "They're almost like a novella," says Shari Anne Brill, director of programming services for Carat, a media advisory firm. "They're stories with a quick beginning, middle and end."

Another reason reality series perform well with younger viewers is that the shows usually revolve around dating or contestants' being voted off. Issues of relationships and rejection resonate with teens.

Teens get special attention from the networks [because] . . . they're trendsetters. "Oftentimes they are the first adopters of a programming breakthrough."

The network of choice among adolescents is Fox, which airs the season's six most popular shows for that age group. One week during the recent February [2003] sweeps period, Fox had all 10 of the highest-rated shows among teens.

"Fox has a fix on younger viewers," says John Rash, director of broadcast negotiations at the Campbell Mithun advertising agency. "That helped propel them to a solid sweeps victory with a younger audience, and bodes well demographically for their future."

According to Gail Berman, Fox's president of entertainment, the key to the network's success isn't just programming content. It's also attitude, a hyperactive, class-clown approach most evident in promos for shows such as "Joe Millionaire."

"We view ourselves as the alternative, irreverent network," Berman says. "And that's very appealing to teens."

The disparity between younger and older viewers is so pronounced that only one traditional scripted series, "Friends," ranks in the top 10 for both teens and the overall TV audience.

That's a remarkable accomplishment for the NBC sitcom, given that its creators and executive producers, Marta Kaufmann and David Crane, say they pay no attention to demographics.

"I have kids," Kaufmann says. "They're good barometers. But I rarely think of them when we're working on an episode." Adds Crane: "Maybe the shows that try to attract younger demos are working too hard to accomplish that. If you set out to be hip, you're going to be anything but."

Though teens are quick on the draw with a remote in hand, when they do find a program they like, they tend to form strong and lasting bonds.

"They're real 'appointment' viewers, tuning in week in and week out," Fox's Berman says. "A show becomes an emotional experience for them, and an emotional commitment."

Yet, for the teen-targeting networks—notably Fox, the WB, and UPN—that very loyalty poses a problem.

Teens always want something new

"You really have to be on your toes if you're the adopted network for that age group," says Tom Bierbaum, NBC's director of ratings. "You can't put on a show and leave it there for 10 years, because the bulk of your audience starts aging out of your demographic. You have to keep recruiting from the bottom end of the teen spectrum."

The difficulty of refreshing a young audience is exemplified by "Beverly Hills 90210." The series aired for nearly a decade on Fox, thanks to devoted fans who grew a little older with each season. But their younger brothers and sisters never adopted Brenda and Dylan.

A recent casualty of that aging process is "Dawson's Creek" on the WB.

"It was huge out of the box with teen viewers," says Mary Hall, the network's senior vice president of research. "The teens that started with it stayed with it. But we haven't gotten a load of new teens." As a result, "Dawson's Creek" will have its finale on May 14 [2003], after five seasons. (It doesn't help that star James Van Der Beek is starting to look older than Fox News' Bill O'Reilly.)

The exception to this trend is the WB's "7th Heaven," which owes its evergreen popularity among teens to its premise. In the sprawling Camden family, there's always a new kid to showcase.

"When the show started, it was all about Matt and Mary," Hall says. "Now it's Simon, played by David Gallagher. He's the hot teen idol. That's how they're able to reload the teen pipeline."

Another difference between younger and older viewers is the way they use the TV.

If you're an adult who grew up with only a handful of stations, you're hemmed in by an invisible fence. Research has repeatedly shown that mature viewers subconsciously stay among the channels with the lowest numerical assignments.

Teens know no such borders. "The younger you are, the more aware you are of the channels that aren't at the bottom of the dial," NBC's Bierbaum says. "Kids are more likely to be zapping up and down the whole cable spectrum."

Partly as a result, prime-time network viewership among teens dropped during the last seven seasons by nearly two million, to a 3.2 million nightly average last season [2002], according to Nielsen Media Research. However, that audience is projected to increase slightly this season [2003], thanks largely to the "reality" boom.

The broadcast networks still run the biggest game in town. The prime-time audiences for the Cartoon Network, Nickelodeon and MTV—the three most popular cable channels among 12- to 17-year-olds—averaged less than 170,000 teen viewers each during the February [2003] "sweeps." In comparison, Fox's "American Idol" is averaging 2.7 million teens per episode this season [2003].

The most sought-after age group for advertisers—because of its disposable income and free-spending ways—has always been 18- to 49-year-olds. But in certain product categories—movies, soda and cosmetics, to name a few—teens are highly prized.

First, though, you have to get them to tune in.

Not only are younger viewers resistant to traditional network offerings, they also watch much less TV than adults.

According to a recent leisure-time study conducted by MTV Networks, 12- to 17-year-olds devote an average of 20 to 22 hours a week to TV viewing. Adults ages 18 to 49 average 32 hours in front of the set. And viewers 50 and older watch the most of all: 42 hours a week.

The elusiveness of teens only makes them more desirable to sponsors.

"There's an ironic inverse relationship," NBC's Bierbaum says. "If you watch less, you become more valuable, because the networks have to work harder to deliver you to the advertisers."

Another reason teens get special attention from the networks is that they're trendsetters.

"Oftentimes they are the first adopters of a programming breakthrough," Bierbaum says. "For instance, 10 years ago teens really took to 'The Real World' on MTV. Now they're 25 and likely to be watching reality programming. They're great detectors."

When one of the older-skewing networks does put on a show that hits with young people, the effects on its audience composition can be dramatic. "When 'Survivor' came on the air," MTV Networks' Frank says, "people were shocked because it immediately lowered CBS' median age by several years—probably a whole generation."

One facet of teen viewing should hearten parents: Among 12- to 17-year-olds' 25 most popular shows this season, only one, ABC's "Celebrity Mole: Hawaii," has begun after 9 P.M. EST. So, presumably, at least teens are getting enough sleep.

15

Reality TV Encourages Young People to Develop Eating Disorders

Sid Kirchheimer

*Sid Kirchheimer is a health and medical writer and editor. He has writ-
ten or edited thirteen books, including* The Doctors Book of Home
Remedies II, *and has served as an editorial director for InteliHealth.com
and as editor in chief for two websites serving ophthalmic professionals.*

Reality TV series that emphasize physical beauty, such as ABC's
Are You Hot?, present unrealistic expectations that may put young
viewers, especially teenage girls, in jeopardy. Their message is that
only thin women are beautiful, which can encourage emotionally
vulnerable teens to develop eating disorders. Parents must be
aware of what their teenagers are watching on television so that
they can help them develop a healthy self-image independent of
media hype.

First there were *The Bachelor, The Bachelorette,* and *Joe Millionaire*—shows
that seemingly ignore the necessities for matrimonial bliss in exchange for Nielsen ratings—and quite successfully. Now new concerns are
emerging over one of the latest "reality" television shows and potential
eating disorders.

In *Are You Hot? The Search for America's Sexiest People,* a parade of eye
candy displays well-sculpted pecs and perky breasts before celebrity
judges, who then detail the contestants' not-so-apparent physical flaws.
Entertaining perhaps, but some say this ABC show hits at the emotional
health of those who are particularly vulnerable—teens and others prone
to eating disorders.

"Individuals on this show are basically deciding that they're going to
trade 10 minutes on TV for a fair amount of emotional mistreatment, but
they're adults and are welcome to choose to do that. I'm concerned more
about the people who watch it, because the show's theme that seems to
get played out is what is really important in life is how you look," says

Sid Kirchheimer, "Reality TV Triggers Health Issues," www.webmd.com, February 28, 2003.

psychologist Randall Flanery, PhD, director of the eating disorders program at the Saint Louis University School of Medicine. "People on this show are proposing they look pretty good and from what I've seen, they do, yet many still wind up getting trashed."

Flanery tells WebMD he's especially concerned about its teenage viewers, who are particularly vulnerable to the cultural ideal in this and other media that suggests the only way to look good is to be thin. "This show isn't alone, but it especially reinforces the idea that if you're not thin, you're a failure and if things aren't going right in your life, it's because you're not thin."

The quest for thinness is dangerous

That, he says, is a recipe for eating disorders such as bulimia and anorexia nervosa, which affect some 8 million Americans—primarily teenage girls and young women.

"There is research suggesting that females who spend more time looking at thin models and comparing themselves to these models are more likely to be dissatisfied with how they look and are more committed to weight loss," Flanery tells WebMD. "This is especially true for girls between ages 13 and 18, who are trying to determine their self-identity and form the person they want to become."

Holly Hoff, program director of the National Eating Disorders Association, also has concerns about the new show, though concedes she hasn't watched it.

Teenage viewers . . . are particularly vulnerable to the cultural ideal in [reality TV] and other media that suggests the only way to look good is to be thin.

"The objectification of individuals based on their looks places a really unfortunate overemphasis on determining people's value and appeal based solely on their appearance," she tells WebMD. "And that sets up pressure that could be part of a very dangerous downward spiral. Girls in this country are literally dying to be thin, since anorexia has the highest death rate of any psychiatric disorder. And we know when people set out to try [to] emulate these most often unhealthy and unattainable standards that they're seeing on shows like this, they go to drastic eating and exercise behaviors that aren't necessarily healthy for them."

So what can parents do—especially in light of a new study, in the March [2003] issue of the *Personality and Social Psychology Bulletin*, that finds people typically pay close attention to their own and others' attractiveness?

"Communicate with your kids on what they are watching and why," says Hoff, whose association serves as a non-profit clearinghouse for information about eating disorders. "Parents need to find out if their children are watching this show and want to look like that, where does this come from? Do they think it will make them more socially accepted? Are they concerned about their body size and shape? Do they really have a weight issue that should be addressed?"

Or follow the advice of Flanery, the father of 10: "Be assertive and say, 'This is a bad show and when I'm in the house, you don't watch it.' More importantly, parents need to stress to their kids that it's not as important how they look as how they treat other people, their values, and what they do with their life."

Both ABC Television spokeswoman Susan Sewell and *Are You Hot?* publicist Pat Breblick declined comment.

16
Young Women Learn Harmful Gender Stereotypes from Reality TV

Susan J. Douglas

Susan J. Douglas is a contributing editor for In These Times, *a national news and opinion magazine.*

Feminists, male and female, find reality TV shows such as *The Bachelor* repulsive because they embody the patriarchal concept that men define womanhood. For example, the woman the bachelor finally chooses from a field of twenty-five contestants supposedly represents the ideal female to viewers, most of whom are young women. Typically, the women viewers identify with and root for their favorite contestant. They hope that the bachelor likes her too, and his choice validates their concept of womanhood. Whether the bachelor agrees with them or not, it is his choice—not theirs—that determines what kind of femininity ensures survival in a world run by men. Thus, reality TV shows such as *The Bachelor* help perpetuate patriarchy.

Any feminist, female or male, who has seen ABC's *The Bachelor* was repulsed. For those who have missed this fine media offering, a carefully selected lunk of a guy—in the most recent case, Aaron—is presented with a harem of 25 also carefully selected young women, all slim, all conventionally pretty and most blonde.

After sampling all the wares, he rejects them one by one until he has chosen the one he likes best. It's not unlike a 4-H competition of prize heifers, except the women weigh less and get to go to fancy resorts. Nor is it unlike the inspections in 19th-century slave pens, except that the women are mostly white, privileged and, I'm sorry to report, there of their own free will.

Women who railed against the sexism of the Miss America pageant, TV detective shows and Mr. Clean commercials in the early '70s must not believe what they are seeing. Feminism aside, the notion that anyone would select the person they're going to marry in six weeks of fantasy dates in hot tubs televised to millions of people is creepy.

Nothing from the real world that binds people together or makes them fight like Rottweilers—religion, politics, money, racial attitudes, child-rearing practices, whether you squeeze the toothpaste from the end or the middle—is allowed to enter this fantasy world. Human relationships are depoliticized here, reinforcing the notion that women and marriage are, and should be, outside the realm of citizenship and civic culture.

Worst of all, the show has been a smash among young women. The demographic group most prized by advertisers, women ages 18 to 34, have made *The Bachelor* a huge hit and prompted worries about the survival of its competition over on NBC, *The West Wing*. From dawn till dusk, ABC's chat room has been abuzz with postings from avid fans. So, as a crotchety, 50-something feminist, I want to know what the hell has happened to this generation of young women?

[Young women] flock to The Bachelor *. . . because they want to participate in a process that reinforces what kinds of femininity ensure survival . . . in a world still run by men.*

Of course, as soon as I ask that, an admonition I have always raised nags at me: If young women en masse are embracing a media offering, then we need to figure out why. Just as Madonna in her boy-toy phase and the Spice Girls with their Wonder-Bras and mini-skirts spoke to millions of girls and young women about what has come to be called "girl power," *The Bachelor*'s popularity tells us something about post-feminism and how young women experience their situations within, yes—I'll use the word—patriarchy.

So I turned to an invaluable source, my teen-age daughter and her friends. My daughter loves the show, and loathes watching it with me, because my stream of invective makes it hard for her to follow what's going on. But here's what I hear these girls saying: They know the show is sexist. (They naively counter that since ABC is going to run *The Bachelorette* in the winter, the network isn't sexist.) Many of them do not find Aaron—an amiable, tall, sandy-haired guy with not much light behind his eyes—all that desirable.

But for them, the show is not about Aaron, it's about the 25 young women. Female viewers see an array of personas, identifying with some and rejecting others, as they calibrate what kind of woman succeeds in a world where appearance and personality still powerfully determine a woman's fate. Helene, the one Aaron finally chose, was enormously popular with young women—the chat room confirms this—because she was cast as "the smart one." Confident, with a sense of humor, Helene was also not overly adulatory of The Man, unlike some of the other contestants. My daughter and her friends did not like the contestants who were wimpy and needy, air-headed, manipulative, untrustworthy, backstabbing or bitchy.

The show, in essence, offers highly normative female "types" into which most women allegedly fall and ropes viewers into damning certain behaviors while applauding others. Thus girls are urged to place themselves on a post-feminist scale of femininity to determine how far they have to go to please men without losing all shreds of their own identity and dignity. In the process, young women calibrate, for better and for worse, what kind of female traits are most likely to ensure success in a male-dominated world.

Patriarchy has been humanized

But Aaron is being judged, too. The show is a metaphor for the persistence—dare I say, desirability—of patriarchy, but in post-feminist clothing. With all of Aaron's faux soul-searching about people needing to be honest and sensitive and not wanting to hurt any woman's feelings, he embodies the lie that patriarchy ain't so bad now because it has been humanized by women.

Viewers tuned in to see if he would confirm girls' worst suspicions that men (and, by extension, a patriarchal system) go for superficial qualities and women who stay in their place—or whether he would embody the new and improved sensitive-new-age-guy patriarchy, the kind that supposedly "gets it." His choice of Helene confirms the latter.

Now it is true that many young women loathe this show and find it completely degrading to women. But millions don't. They flock to *The Bachelor* in part because they want to participate in a process that reinforces what kinds of femininity ensure survival, and what kinds do not, in a world still run by men. In so doing, they become complicit in perpetuating an ethic from the '50s: that women be judged first and foremost by their bodies, faces and personality traits, rather than their brains, integrity, courage, talents or, heaven forbid, political convictions.

17

Korea Takes a Dim View of Reality TV

Korea Herald

The Korea Herald *is one of the leading English-language dailies in Asia. The newspaper carries selected news and opinion pieces as well as science stories from the* New York Times, Los Angeles Times, *and* Washington Post. *It also has a news exchange agreement with the* Japan Times *and the* China Daily.

Reality TV is not yet well accepted in Korea. Because Koreans emphasize family ties rather than independence, they are not as interested in watching the details of individual lives as are Americans, who value individualism. Further, state censorship, a morality standard based on Confucianism, tight network budgets, and a lack of familiarity with this very Western genre are all barriers to Koreans' acceptance of reality TV. Ethical broadcasting standards and a Korean law that prohibits airing details about other people's lives without their consent also make it difficult to broadcast reality TV shows in Korea.

Reality TV is marauding the West, infiltrating Asia and hitting a brick wall in Korea. In the face of censorship, Confucianism, crippling budgets and collective unfamiliarity with the not-so-new genre, Korean producers from the nation's three terrestrial Goliaths, KBS, SBS and MBC, indicate that there is at present neither a niche nor timetable for "those kind of shows."

Those kinds of shows tend to be restricted to Cable. Fox's "Joe Millionaire" rides on the back of a public joke at the expense of female participants vying for the attention of phony playboy slash construction worker Evan Marriott. Forty million viewers switched on when he admitted the truth to the "lucky" girl. CBS's "Survivor" is in the Amazon for its sixth inning while "Big Brother" is demonizing its third group of 10 housemates.

Routine characteristics of these shows involve contestants being voted out by the viewing public and, in the U.S. versions, cashing in with up to a million bucks. The pipeline is now bulging with U.K. Channel 4's "Wife Swap," Fox's "Married by America" and "The Real Beverly Hillbillies," with CBS scouting for a rural clan who can look forward to 12 months of being the butt of the next national joke.

Asia has only just dipped its toe in the Reality TV pool. China's "Journey to Shangri-la" is effectively a localized "Survivor" with the communist forefathers replacing the cash jackpot with an ideological zeroing-in on teamwork as opposed to competition. Taiwan-based Star followed suit with plans to make their own "Temptation Island" (a kind of set up mating game) but then shelved the project indefinitely.

"Western people live in a more individual-based society, so they are interested in watching other individual's lives. Koreans prefer family ties to independence."

Hong Kong has gone gung-ho with game show fever, importing shows like "Who Wants to Be a Millionaire." Japan remains hell-bent on airing horrifically cruel game shows. In one such outing, viewers get to see advertisers buy their airtime by trading seconds on TV for seconds spent in tubs of boiling water.

Does gadget-loving, comic book reading, Starcraft-obsessed Asia relish games more than spying on other people?

MBC Project Manager Kim Ji-su disclosed that the Korean station sent out feelers for a Big Brother or Survivor-style program, but dropped the idea at the planning stage due to negative feedback. He points the finger at Confucianism, saying the legacy of designated family roles makes collective "peeping" an uncomfortable experience.

The channel gets its ratings from humanitarian documentaries, such as the recent MBC Special about a North Korean defector, and daily dramas like "Mermaid" that focus on nuclear family relationships. Kim decodes their popularity, and Reality TV's miscarriage, to a hemispheric social gulf.

Family ties vs. independence

"Western people live in a more individual-based society, so they are interested in watching other individuals' lives. Koreans prefer family ties to independence," he said.

On SBS the closest thing to a reality show is "Oh My God!" plugged as "the world's funniest videos" and crammed with melodramatic pet rescues. Producer Jung Ji-wong says none of the stations have budgets to cover expensive reality shows and what they do have is markedly less intrusive. He cites an old program, "Hidden Camera," which was popular but heavily criticized for spying on celebrities and tripping them up on film.

The Korea Broadcasting Committee's Kim Young-su reports that reality programs have the potential to break the law. "Article 19 says we can't broadcast people's private lives without their consent," he says.

The ethics codes prevent KBS's Lee Young-don from replicating shows like NBC's "Fear Factor," which puts celebrities in dangerous situations like a snake pit, or covers them in cockroaches. Such gruesome outings have no immediate future in Korea because, "the ethics board will come down on them and so terrestrial television producers are reluctant to go near them," he said.

However, KBS does air a couple of reality shows on Sunday mornings. At 9:30 A.M. KBS 2 broadcasts "Challenge World Expedition." Celebrities are immersed in foreign cultures or remote locations, such as an African village, or get to spend a few days as a Formula 1 driver. This brand of role-reversal Reality TV is steadily carving a space for itself.

MTV Korea has found a middle ground with "Tim's World," which debunks myths and shadows Tim on his road to stardom. "It is the first Reality TV show to be aired by the station. The format is unique compared to other broadcasts in Korea," heralds employee Lee Kang-sup.

Until Tim gets a girlfriend and the camera crew rappels through his bedroom window, everything will be fine. As long as Reality TV documents the right side of reality, it'll get through.

Organizations to Contact

The editors have compiled the following list of organizations concerned with issues debated in this book. The descriptions are derived from materials provided by the organizations. All have publications or information available for interested readers. The list was compiled on the date of publication of the present volume; the information provided here may change. Be aware that many organizations take several weeks or longer to respond to inquiries, so allow as much time as possible.

American Psychological Association (APA)
Office of Public Affairs
750 First St. NE, Washington, DC 20002-4242
(202) 336-5700
e-mail: public.affairs@apa.org • website: www.apa.org

This society of psychologists aims to "advance psychology as a science, as a profession, and as a means of promoting human welfare." Although it believes that viewing television violence can have potential dangers for children, it opposes the creation of an age-based television ratings system. APA produces numerous publications, including "Children and Television Violence" and "APA Denounces Proposed Age-Based Television Rating System."

Friends of Canadian Broadcasting
Box 200/238, 131 Bloor St. West, Toronto, ON M5S 1R8 Canada
fax: (416) 968-7406
e-mail: friends@friendscb.ca • website: www.friendscb.ca/contacts.htm

Friends of Canadian Broadcasting is a Canada-wide voluntary organization whose mission is to defend and enhance the quality and quantity of Canadian programming in the Canadian audiovisual system. The organization supports public policy initiatives, public opinion leadership, and research activities. It offers a variety of resources, including press releases, policy briefs, and fact sheets.

Media Research Center (MRC)
113 S. West St., 2nd Fl., Alexandria, VA 22314
(703) 683-9733
e-mail: mrc@mediaresearch.org • website: www.mrc.org

The center is a conservative media watchdog organization concerned with what it perceives to be a liberal bias in the news and entertainment media. In 1995 it opened the Parents Television Council to bring family programming back to television. MRC publishes the monthly newsletters *Media Watch* and *Notable Quotables*.

Morality in the Media (MIM)
475 Riverside Dr., Suite 239, New York, NY 10115
(212) 870-3222 • fax: (212) 870-2765
e-mail: mimnyc@ix.netcom.com • website: www.moralityinmedia.org

Established in 1962, MIM is a national, not-for-profit interfaith organization that works to combat obscenity and to uphold decency standards in the media. It maintains the National Obscenity Law Center, a clearinghouse of legal materials, and conducts public information programs to involve concerned citizens. It publishes the *Morality in Media Newsletter* and the handbook *TV: The World's Greatest Mind-Bender.*

National Coalition on Television Violence (NCTV)
5132 Newport Ave., Bethesda, MD 20816
e-mail: reach@nctvv.org • website: www.nctvv.org

NCTV is a research and education association dedicated to reducing the violence in films and television programming. It distributes ratings, reviews, and violence research. It publishes the quarterly *NCTV News* as well as various reports and educational materials.

Parents Television Council (PTC)
7905 Hollywood Blvd., #1010, Hollywood, CA 90028
(213) 621-2506
website: www.parentstv.org

PTC was founded in 1995 as the Hollywood project of the Media Research Center. It publishes special reports focusing on a variety of topics relating to the content of primetime television—including in-depth analyses of the family hour and the new television rating system. It publishes the *Family Guide to Prime Time Television.*

Society for the Eradication of Television (SET)
Box 10491, Oakland, CA 94610-0491
(510) 763-8712

SET members oppose television and encourage others to stop all television viewing. The society believes television "retards the inner life of human beings, destroys human interaction, and squanders time." SET maintains a speakers bureau and reference library and publishes manuals and pamphlets, the periodic *Propaganda War Comix*, and the quarterly *SET Free: The Newsletter Against Television.*

TV-FreeAmerica
1611 Connecticut Ave. NW, Suite 3A, Washington, DC 20009
(202) 887-0436 • fax: (202) 518-5560
e-mail: tvfa@essential.org • website: www.tvfa.org

TV-FreeAmerica is a national nonprofit organization that encourages Americans to reduce the amount of television they watch in order to promote stronger families and communities. It sponsors the National TV-Turnoff Week, when more than 5 million people across the country go without television for seven days. It publishes the quarterly newsletter the *TV-Free American.*

Website

Reality Television
website: www.realitytv.org

Reality Television is a website devoted to the reality TV genre. It includes links to other websites, articles, and a forum where individual programs and program participants are discussed. It also features specific pages for each reality TV series.

Bibliography

Books

Mark Andrejevic   *Reality TV: The Work of Being Watched*. Lanham, MD: Rowman and Littlefield, 2003.

Chuck Barris   *Confessions of a Dangerous Mind: An Unauthorized Autobiography*. New York: Hyperion, 2002.

Sam Brenton and Reuben Cohen   *Shooting People: Adventures in Reality TV*. London and New York: Verso Books, 2003.

Will Brooker and Deborah Jermyn, eds.   *The Audience Studies Reader*. London and New York: Routledge, 2003.

Tim Brooks and Earle Marsh   *The Complete Directory to Prime Time Network and Cable TV Shows*. New York: Ballantine Books, 1999.

Louis Chunovic   *One Foot on the Floor: The Curious Evolution of Sex on Television from* I Love Lucy *to* South Park. New York: TV Books, 2000.

Jon Dovey   *Freakshow: First Person Media and Factual Television*. London and Sterling, VA: Pluto Press, 2000.

James Friedman   *Reality Squared: Televisual Discourse on the Real*. New Brunswick, NJ: Rutgers University Press, 2002.

Kevin Glynn   *Tabloid Culture: Trash Taste, Popular Power, and the Transformation of American Television*. Durham, NC: Duke University Press, 2000.

Matt Hills   *Fan Cultures*. London and New York: Routledge, 2002.

Susan Isaacs   *Brave Dames and Wimpettes: What Women Are Really Doing on Page and Screen*. New York: Ballantine Books, 1999.

Toni Johnson-Woods   *Big Brother: Why Did That Reality-TV Show Become Such a Phenomenon?* St. Lucia, Australia: University of Queensland Press, 2002.

John O'Neill   *Plato's Cave: Television and Its Discontents*. Cresskill, NJ: Hampton Press, 2002.

Cheryl Pawlowski   *Glued to the Tube*. Naperville, IL: Sourcebooks, 2000.

Nat Segaloff   *The Everything TV and Movie Trivia Mini Book*. Avon, MA: Adams Media, 2001.

Ellen Seiter   *Television and New Media Audiences*. Oxford and New York: Clarendon Press, 1999.

Colin Sparks and John Tulloch, eds.   *Tabloid Tales: Global Debates over Media Standards*. Lanham, MD: Rowman and Littlefield, 2000.

Dorothy Collins Swanson   *The Story of Viewers for Quality Television: From Grassroots to Prime Time*. Syracuse, NY: Syracuse University Press, 2000.

John Tulloch   *Watching Television Audiences: Cultural Theories and Methods*. London and New York: Oxford University Press, 2000.

Periodicals

Age   "A Reality Check on Reality TV," July 18, 2001. www.theage.com.

Chuck Barney   "Truth Is, Networks See No Stability with Reality TV," *Contra Costa Times*, January 14, 2003.

Larry Bonko   "Troubled Couples Seek Reality TV," *Virginian-Pilot*, August 10, 2002.

Peter Bowes   "Casting Call for Reality TV Surgery," *BBC News World Edition*, August 14, 2002.

Sasha Brown   "Confessions of a Reality-TV Veteran," *Christian Science Monitor*, March 28, 2003.

Duncan Campbell   "Southerners Rebel over Hillbilly Reality TV Show," *Guardian*, February 12, 2003.

Darva Conger and Rick Rockwell   "TV's Reality Check," *People Weekly*, March 6, 2000.

Michelle Conlin   "America's Reality—TV Addiction," *Business Week Online*, January 30, 2003. www.businessweek.com

Alisha Davis   "Reality TV Dominates the Airwaves," *CNN.com*, January 23, 2003. www.cnn.com.

Andy Dehnart   "*The Real World* Refuses to Grow Up," *Salon.com*, July 3, 2001. www.salon.com.

Andy Dehnart   "Whither Reality TV," *Salon.com*, October 3, 2001. www.salon.com.

Economist   "The Reality After the Show," September 14, 2002.

Gloria Goodale   "The Reality of Real TV: It Comes in Cycles," *Christian Science Monitor*, February 2, 2001.

Tim Goodman   "It's Time to Get Real About Reality TV," *San Francisco Chronicle*, January 20, 2003.

Ronald Grover   "For CBS, *Survivor* Is a Strategy—and a Fountain of Youth," *Business Week Online*, June 20, 2000. www.businessweek.com.

Andrew Gumbel   "Rumbles in the Reality TV Jungle," *Independent*, March 13, 2002.

Carla Hay   "*American Idol* Weds Reality TV and Music," *Billboard*, August 3, 2002.

Reynolds Holding   "Litigious Reality Behind Reality TV," *San Francisco Chronicle*, March 23, 2003.

Tonya Jameson — "Publicity's the Real Prize on Reality TV," *Charlotte Observer*, January 19, 2001.

Mary Lynn F. Jones — "No Difference," *American Prospect*, January 10, 2003.

Dave Karger — "Reality TV: Performance Anxiety," *Entertainment Weekly*, March 17, 2003.

Todd Leopold — "How Much Reality TV Can We Survive?" *CNN.com*, May 1, 2001. www.cnn.com.

Gary Levin — "How Real Is Reality TV?" *USA Today*, March 3, 2001.

Charlie McCollum — "The Show That Spawned Reality TV Begins Its 10th Season," *San Jose Mercury News*, July 2, 2001.

Fred McKissack — "Enough Reality Already," *Progressive*, September 2000.

Chris Mooney — "Surviving Pop Culture, Conservatives Drown Trying to Sink *Survivor*," *American Prospect*, August 29, 2000.

Noel Neff — "The Fame Game," *Know Your World Extra*, November 30, 2001.

Doug Nye — "How Much Longer Can People Stomach TV's Reality Junk Food?" *State*, January 13, 2003.

Cathrine Orenstein — "Reality TV Today's Fairy Tales," *Seattle Post-Intelligencer*, March 14, 2003.

Ken Parish Perkins — "Reality TV Craze Keeps Hollywood Writers Idle," *Star-Telegram*, September 11, 2000.

Dick Polman — "Fox Stretching Reality—Plans TV Game Show on Presidential Race," *Philadelphia Inquirer*, January 24, 2003.

Anna Quindlen — "Are You Hot? Is It Nuclear?" *Newsweek*, February 24, 2003.

Anna Quindlen — "Watching the World Go By," *Newsweek*, February 26, 2001.

Lynette Rice — "When Reality Attacks," *Entertainment Weekly*, March 17, 2003.

Beth Rowen — "The History of Reality TV," *Infoplease.com*, July 21, 2002. www.infoplease.com.

Marie-Laure Ryan — "From the *Truman Show* to *Survivor*: Narrative Versus Reality in Fake and Real Reality TV," *Intensities*, Autumn/Winter 2001.

George Saunders — "My Guilty Pleasures," *New Yorker*, February 2, 2003.

Michael Seeber — "The Search for Survivors," *Psychology Today*, September/October 2001.

Ben Shouse — "Reality TV Puts Group Behavior to the Test," *Science*, November 9, 2001.

Betsy Streisand — "Did You Say Reality TV? Or Surreal TV?" *U.S. News & World Report*, January 22, 2001.

Noy Thrupkaew   "Really Real: *Boston 24-7* Could Save Reality TV," *American Prospect*, June 7, 2002.

Dan Vergano   "ER Patients' Privacy at Risk in Reality TV," *USA Today*, July 16, 2002.

Rebecca Waer   "Evangelical Teens to Give Out Their Own Dose of Reality TV," *Christian Times*, March 20, 2002.

Jon Warech   "Extreme Reality Shows Generate Cash—and Lawsuits," *Miami Herald*, March 12, 2003.

Joanne Weintraub   "The Year in Review: *Idol* Worship Is Part of TV's Reality," *Milwaukee Journal Sentinel*, December 23, 2002.

Cintra Wilson   "Survival of the Vilest," *Salon.com*, June 14, 2000. www.salon.com.

Karl Zinmeister   "Taking Out the TV Trash," *American Enterprise*, March/April 1999.

Index

television
  changes in societal values and, 9–10
  coverage of Iraq war by, 22–24
  viewing habits
    of teens, 54, 56–57
Temptation Island (TV series), 17, 46, 52
Terreri, Jill, 34
Thompson, Robert, 10, 11, 18, 41, 43
TruthQuest (TV series), 34

Van Doren, Charles, 49

War of the Worlds (radio drama), 49
Washington Post (newspaper), 13
Welles, Orson, 49
Wesson, Tina, 33
Wiglesworth, Kelly, 46

Wiltz, James, 25
women, learn harmful gender
  stereotypes from reality TV, 61–63

Yates, Donald, 50
youth
  are taught about life through reality
    TV, 52–54
  identify with issues presented by
    reality TV, 54–57
  learn harmful gender stereotypes from
    reality TV, 61–63
  reality TV encourages development of
    eating disorders in, 58–60
  viewing habits of, 54, 56–57

Zohn, Ethan, 31–32